Beaded Critters

SONAL BHATT

Sterling Publishing Co., Inc.
New York

To my loving family, including my new
friend Ian and especially my Mom.

Photography by Michael Hnatov
Bead drawings by the author
Edited by Isabel Stein
Design by Rose Sheifer

Library of Congress Cataloging-in-Publication Data

Bhatt, Sonal.
  Beaded critters / Sonal Bhatt.
    p. cm.
  Includes index.
  ISBN 1-4027-0416-X
  1. Beadwork—Juvenile literature. 2. Animals in art—Juvenile literature.
I. Title.

TT860.B4896 2005
745.58'2—dc22

                                                    2004028504

10 9 8 7 6 5 4 3 2 1

Published by Sterling Publishing Co., Inc.
387 Park Avenue South, New York, NY 10016
©2005 by Sonal Bhatt
Distributed in Canada by Sterling Publishing
^c/o Canadian Manda Group, 165 Dufferin Street
Toronto, Ontario, Canada M6K 3H6
Distributed in Great Britain and Europe by Chris Lloyd at Orca Book
Services, Stanley House, Fleets Lane, Poole BH15 3AJ, England
Distributed in Australia by Capricorn Link (Australia) Pty. Ltd.
P.O. Box 704, Windsor, NSW 2756, Australia

Sterling ISBN 1-4027-0416-X

Contents

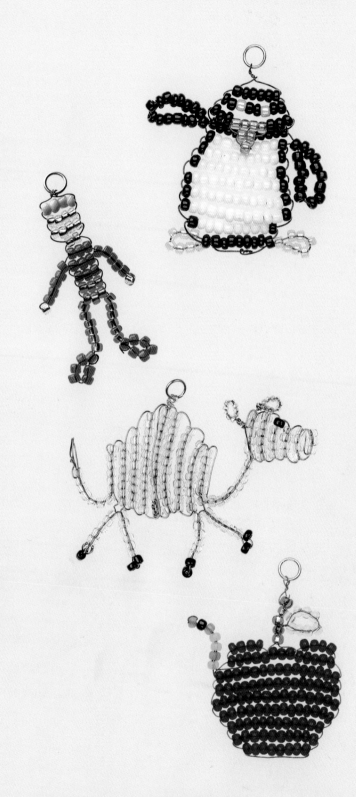

The Basics

Are you ready to make some beaded friends? They sparkle, they shine. Beaded critters are fun to make. Who knows? You may make yourself a good luck charm! Whether you use it for a keychain, an ornament, a pony-tail holder, a gift tag, a window decoration, a backpack tag, or simply to have a new beaded friend, you will have lots of fun making each critter in this book.

For centuries, people around the world have had favorite animals. In ancient Egypt, seahorses were believed to be guides that would help boaters travel safely down the Nile. Many people around the world carry ladybugs as good luck charms. What animals do you think will bring you luck or be fun to make? In this book you will learn to make many critters. Try them all, and create a beaded collection. So let's not waste time; let's get started with the basics of beaded critters. All of the supplies that you will need can be found in arts and crafts stores. If you can't find anything listed below on your own, don't be afraid to ask for help.

e beads

Beads

First, let's talk about beads. For the projects in this book, we will be using mostly e beads. E beads are also known as size 6° or 6/0 round glass or plastic beads. They are about 4 mm in diameter, about the size of a peppercorn. If you were to line them up, you could fit 6 beads along an inch (2.5 cm). They are also sometimes called small pony beads. E beads come in many different colors. Don't worry if you don't have the right color bead. If you can't find the colors shown for the patterns in the book, use your imagination and substitute the colors you have.

Some patterns use seed beads. Seed beads are smaller than e beads. They come in several sizes. For the size we used, there are about 17 seed beads to an inch (7 per cm).

For one or two projects you will need a large bead about 1'' (2.5 cm) in diameter. These will be described in the projects where they are used.

As you are beading, you will find that keeping your beads in small bowls is a good way to keep them from rolling away. You should also spread a towel under you as you work to catch beads that you might drop. This way, you won't lose any of your beads.

Wire

To string the beads, you will need wire that fits through each bead at least twice. The wire needs to be easy to bend, but not so thin that it won't hold its shape. The best wire for this is 26-gauge; the 26 refers to the thickness of the wire. You can find this wire in a number of colors. Experiment with using different colors of wire. Try some that match the beads you are using in the critters you make.

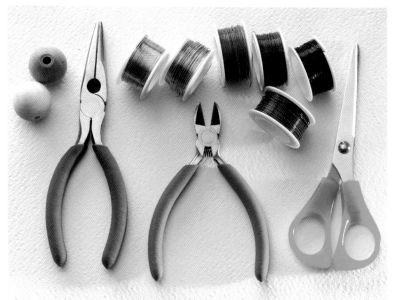

Left to right: 1"(2.5 cm) beads, pliers, wire cutters, scissors.

Jump rings

Tools

You will need wire cutters or scissors to cut the wire lengths you will be using. A ruler or measuring tape will also be useful to measure pieces of wire. You might want to have a set of long-nose pliers that will help you pull the wire through the beads to make your rows of beads neater.

Attachments

Each of the beaded critters is attached to a jump ring. Jump rings are used at the ends of necklaces and bracelets and may be made of steel, copper, or more expensive metals. A jump ring is a strong hoop of wire that has a cut in it. It doesn't bend easily. Jump rings come in various sizes. Choose the size of jump ring based on the width of the attachment you will use for the beaded critter. If the attachment is something thick, you need a wide jump ring. You will find the jump ring is helpful. Once you have a jump ring on your beaded critter, you can attach your beaded critter to other hardware. Then your beaded critter will be ready to attach to your backpack, keychain, hair elastic, ponytail holder, or necklace.

A few attachments for your beaded critters are shown in the photos.

Attaching a Jump Ring

Many of the patterns in this book start with a jump ring. To attach one, you need to string your wire through the jump ring. Practice attaching a jump ring to a wire using the following directions. Then you will know what to do when it asks you to attach a wire to a jump ring in the patterns.

1. First fold a 10'' (25 cm) wire in half (Fig. 1).

Figure 1

2. Put the folded end of the wire a little way through the jump ring (Fig. 2).

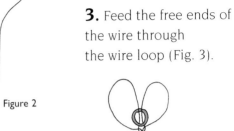

Figure 2

3. Feed the free ends of the wire through the wire loop (Fig. 3).

Figure 3

4. Pull tight, and you are ready to start beading (Fig. 4).

Figure 4

Key chains and other attachments.

Rows of Beads

Most of the beaded critters are made of rows of beads. Practice making rows of beads so you will know how to do the patterns in this book. Use the piece of wire that you just attached to the jump ring for this exercise.

1. Separate the wire ends. One wire end will be called wire A and the other will be wire B for clarity (Fig. 1).

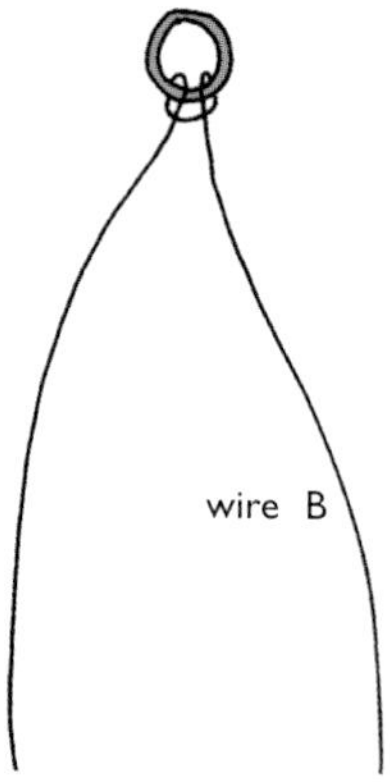

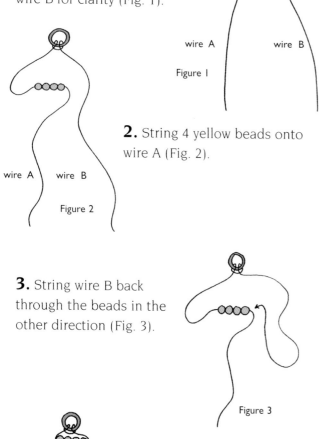

Figure 1

2. String 4 yellow beads onto wire A (Fig. 2).

Figure 2

3. String wire B back through the beads in the other direction (Fig. 3).

Figure 3

4. Pull tight. That completes a row of beads (Fig. 4).

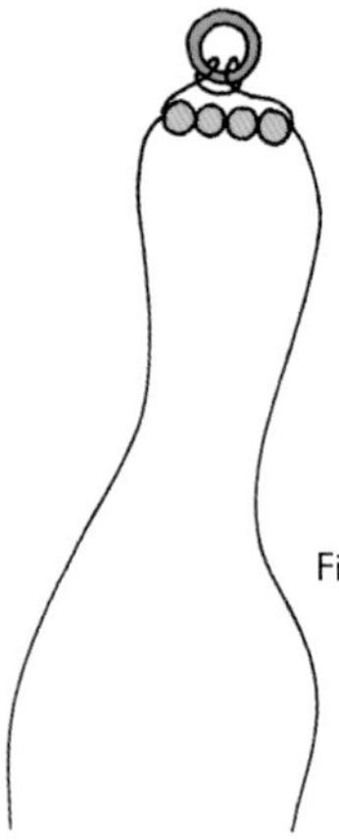

Figure 4

5. String 6 blue beads onto wire A (Fig. 5).

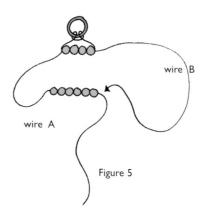

wire B

wire A

Figure 5

6. String wire B back through the 6 blue beads and pull tight. This step will be difficult if your wire is too thick. That completes the next row of beads (Fig. 6).

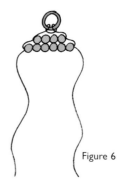

Figure 6

The above is an example of how you will be making rows of beads. Follow each pattern for the color and number of beads to string for each row. We numbered the bead rows in the figures so you can find them easily: r1 = row 1, r2 = row 2, etc. Some critters are worked from the top down, some from the bottom up.

What If I Run Out of Wire?

Say you are in the middle of making a critter and you see that you are running out of wire. Use the same practice piece to which you just added rows, and try this:

1. While you still have some wire left, put the 2 wire ends together. Twist them together 3 or 4 times (Fig. 1).

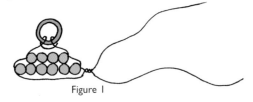

Figure 1

2. Trim off the extra wire (Fig. 2).

Figure 2

3. Add a new length of wire through the last row of beads as shown (Fig. 3). Now you can continue the project.

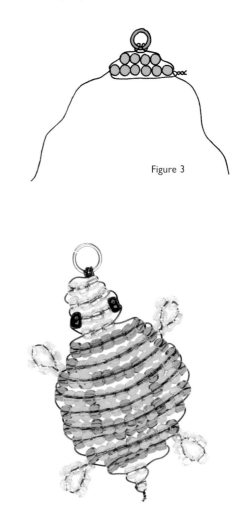

Figure 3

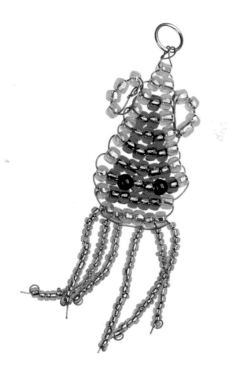

What Do I Do at the End of a Project?

At the end of a project in this book, you may have extra wire left on your critter. Put the wires together, twist the ends together 3 or 4 times, and cut off the extra wire as you did when you were running out of wire. Be sure to tuck under any sharp wire ends so they don't scratch someone.

Choosing a Project

Some projects in this book are very easy for a beginner. Some are more difficult or take longer. To start out with, choose a simple project that has only a few steps. Go on to doing longer, more difficult projects after your first few easy projects. We have coded the projects to guide you. One bead under the title means the project is easy for beginners.

Two beads means the project is for beaders who already have done a few easy projects. Three beads under the title means the project is for advanced beaders.

Be creative! If you didn't find the critter you wanted in this book, try making your own pattern. With all the skills that you will have after making the patterns in the book, you probably will be able to design your own beaded animals. Now that we know the basics, let's get to some beading!

Bunch of Grapes

Grapes are tasty to eat and come in many colors. Try making red, blue, or green grapes too after you finish this project.

You Will Need

- jump ring
- 8" (20 cm) wire
- 19 purple e beads
- 30 green seed beads

This pattern is worked from the bottom point of the grapes up, towards the leaves.

1. Add one purple bead to the center of an 8" wire to make row 1 (Fig. 1).

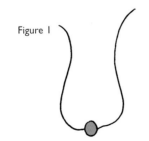

Figure 1

2. Loop the wire back through the bead in the opposite direction as shown (Fig. 2).

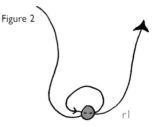

Figure 2

3. String the following rows of e beads (Fig. 3) as explained on page 8):

> row 2: 3 purple
> row 3: 4 purple
> row 4: 5 purple
> row 5: 6 purple

Then put the wire ends together and twist them together (Fig. 3).

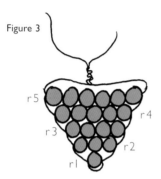

Figure 3

4. To make a leaf, separate the wires and add 15 green seed beads to one wire. After you add the 15 beads, gently bend the wire to form a loop and twist the remaining wire around the base of the loop twice (Fig. 4).

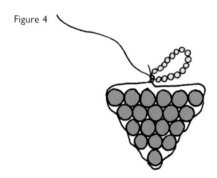

Figure 4

5. Repeat Step 4 on the second wire to make the second leaf (Fig. 5).

Figure 5

6. Put the wires together and twist around the jump ring a few times (Fig. 6). Trim off the extra wire.

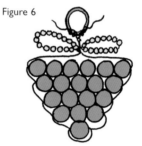

Figure 6

Watermelon Slice

Here's a nice slice of watermelon that won't get juice all over you.

1. Attach a jump ring on the center of the wire (Fig. 1).

Figure 1

2. Then add 1 pink bead to make row 1, by stringing one wire end through the bead and stringing the other wire end back through the bead in the other direction (Fig. 2).

Figure 2

3. String on the following rows of beads (Fig. 3):

row 2: 2 pink
row 3: 4 pink
row 4: 5 pink
row 5: 7 pink
row 6: 1 pink, 1 black, 2 pink, 1 black, 2 pink, 1 black, 1 pink
row 7: 12 pink
row 8: 15 green

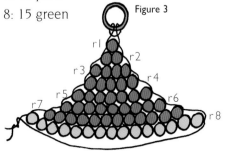

Figure 3

You Will Need

- jump ring
- 10'' (25 cm) wire
- 37 dark pink e beads
- 3 black e beads
- 15 green e beads

4. Twist the wire ends together and trim off the extra wire.

Apple...with Worm

People aren't the only ones who like apples. Here's a nice worm who enjoys one too.

For this pattern, we start from the bottom row and work up.

1. String 8 red beads, centered on the 20″ wire for row 1. Then string the following rows of beads (Fig. 1) so both wire ends go through them, as explained on page 8:

> row 2: 10 red beads
> row 3: 12 red beads
> row 4: 14 red beads
> row 5: 15 red beads
> row 6: 15 red beads
> row 7: 15 red beads

To make the worm, string 5 assorted green beads, 1 black, and 1 green bead onto wire B. Pull the wire over the last bead and string it back through all the other 6 beads (Fig. 1).

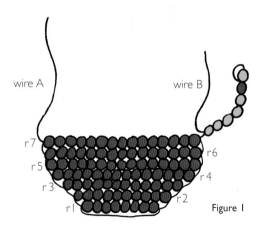

Figure 1

You Will Need

- jump ring (optional)
- 20″ (51 cm) wire
- 110 red e beads
- 5 amber e beads
- 8 light green e beads
- 6 green e beads of assorted shades
- 1 black bead

2. Add row 8, 13 red beads (Fig. 2). Then add 4 red beads to wire A, and string wire A through the central 3 beads (6, 7, 8) of row 8, as shown.

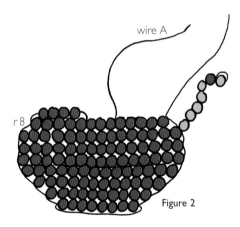

Figure 2

3. Add 4 red beads to wire B (Fig. 3). String wire B through the middle beads (6, 7, 8) of row 8.

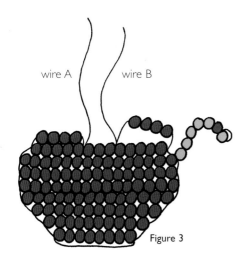

Figure 3

4. Twist wires A and B together and add 2 amber beads (Fig. 4). Separate the wires and add 8 light green beads to wire B, stringing the wire back through the first green bead (Fig. 4). Then put the wires together and add 3 amber beads. Finally, string wire A back through the last bead to secure the beads. Twist the wires around a jump ring and twist again. Trim off the extra wire.

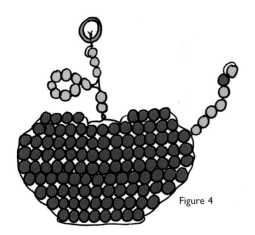

Figure 4

Beaded Boy

This little fellow likes to travel, so put him on your jacket or backpack.

1. Center a jump ring on the wire. We will call one-half wire A. The other half is wire B. Put 4 brown beads on wire A. Run wire B through the beads in the opposite direction to make row 1 (Fig. 1).

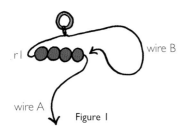

Figure 1

2. Then add the following rows of beads in the same way (Fig. 2):

> row 2: 4 light peach
> row 3: 4 light peach
> row 4: 2 light peach
> row 5: 3 red

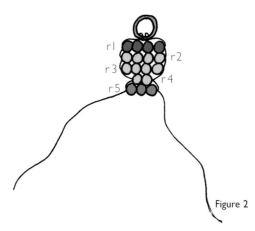

Figure 2

3. To make an arm, add 5 red beads and then 1 light peach bead to wire A. Pull the wire around the peach bead and string it back through all 5 red beads you just added, as shown (Fig. 3). Repeat on wire B.

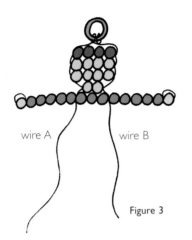

Figure 3

4. Add the following rows of beads (Fig. 4):

     row 6: 3 red
     row 7: 3 red
     row 8: 3 blue
     row 9: 3 blue

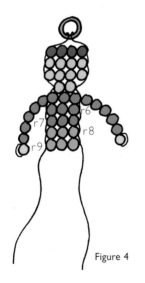

Figure 4

5. To make a leg and foot, add 6 blue beads and then 6 amber beads to wire A. Then string back through the first amber bead you added, as shown (Fig. 5). Repeat on wire B to make the second leg and foot.

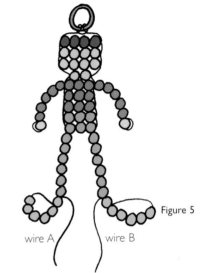

Figure 5

6. To finish the foot, loop wire A back through the first amber bead again to secure the beads (Fig. 6). Repeat on wire B. Trim off the extra wire on both wire A and B.

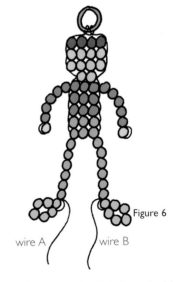

Figure 6

Now that you have made this beaded boy, try changing colors. You can even try to make your beaded boy extra tall by adding in another row of beads!

Beaded Girl

Here's a bouncy beaded girl, ready to accompany you on your adventures.

1. Center a jump ring on the 15" wire. We will call one-half wire A and one-half wire B. String wire A through one brown bead (Fig. 1).

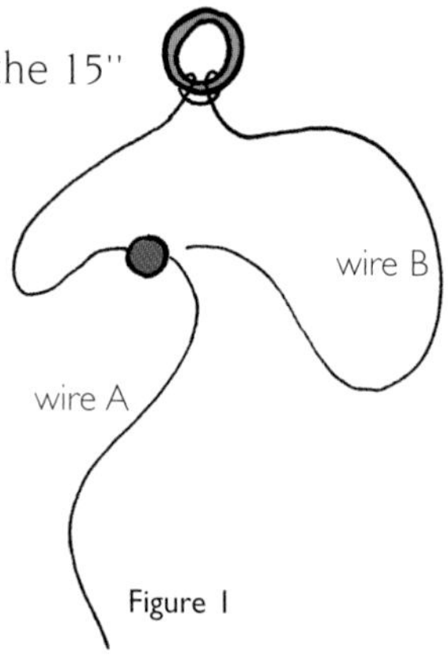

wire B

wire A

Figure 1

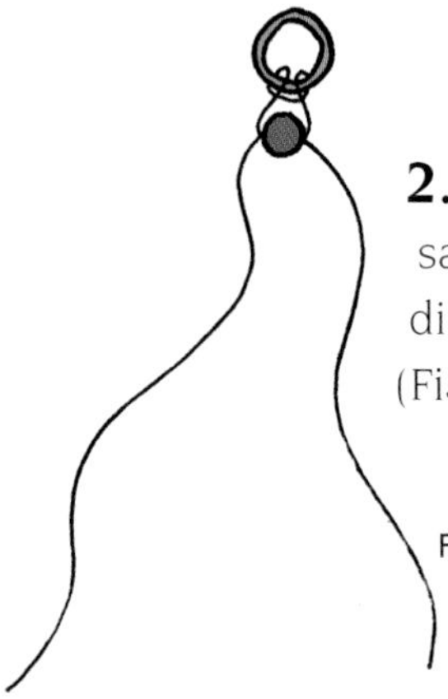

2. String wire B through the same bead in the opposite direction and pull tight (Fig. 2).

Figure 2

3. To make the hair, string 8 brown beads onto one wire. Then string the wire back through all but the outermost bead, as shown (Fig. 3).

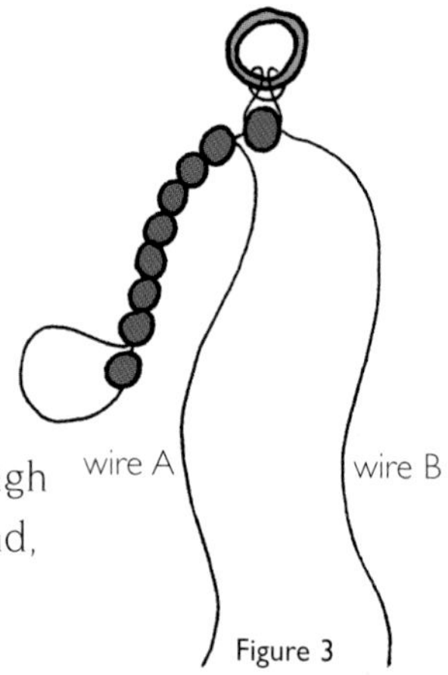

wire A

wire B

Figure 3

You Will Need

- jump ring
- 15" (38 cm) wire
- 17 brown e beads
- 25 gold e beads
- 25 blue e beads
- 17 pink e beads

4. Repeat Step 3 on the other wire to make the second side of the hair. Then string 3 gold beads on one wire and run the second wire back through these beads in the opposite direction to make row 1 (Fig. 4), the start of the face.

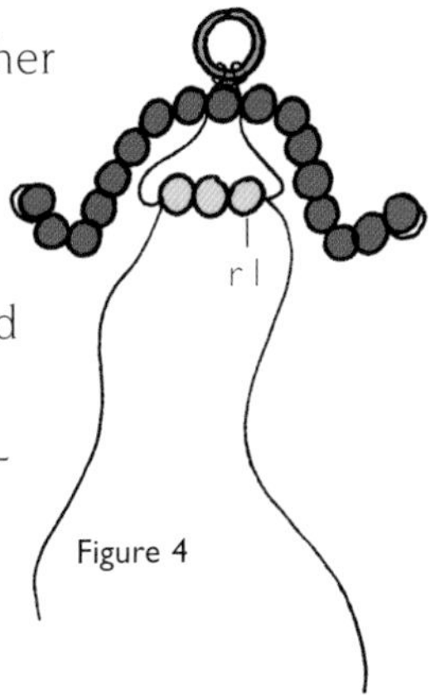

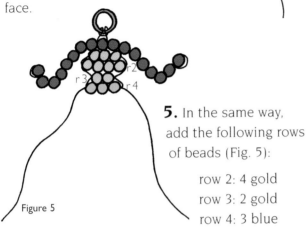

Figure 4

5. In the same way, add the following rows of beads (Fig. 5):

row 2: 4 gold
row 3: 2 gold
row 4: 3 blue

Figure 5

6. To make an arm, add 2 blue and then 4 gold beads to wire A. Then run the wire back through all the beads you just added but the outermost gold bead (Fig. 6). Repeat on the other wire to make the other arm.

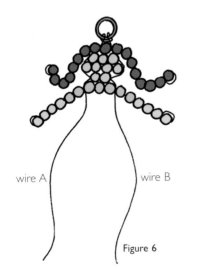

wire A   wire B

Figure 6

7. To make the chest and skirt, add the following rows of beads in the same way (Fig. 7):

row 5: 3 blue
row 6: 3 blue
row 7: 3 pink
row 8: 6 pink
row 9: 8 pink

At the bottom of the skirt (row 9), twist both wires together two times right below the center, as shown in Fig. 7.

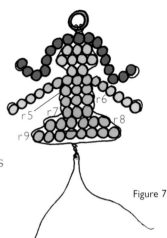

Figure 7

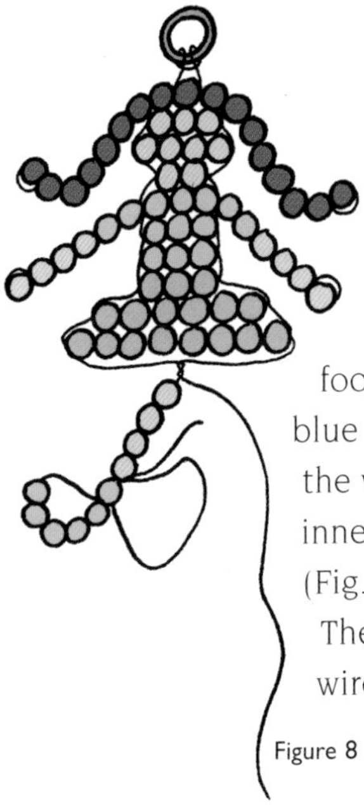

8. To make a leg and a foot, add 4 gold and then 6 blue beads to one wire. String the wire back through the innermost blue bead twice (Fig. 8) to secure the beads. Then trim off the excess wire.

Figure 8

9. Repeat Step 8 on the second wire to make the second leg. The finished beaded girl can be seen in Fig. 9.

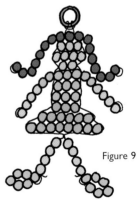

Figure 9

Mermaid

Are mermaids real? From earliest times, sailors have believed that these beautiful creatures, half fish and half human, live in the sea. Your mermaid can live on dry land, on your backpack or jacket.

This pattern starts at the bottom of the mermaid's tail.

1. Fold the wire in the middle. One side will be wire A and the other will be wire B. To start the tail, string 6 green beads on wire A. Then string back through all the beads in the same direction with wire A (Fig. 1).

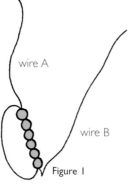

Figure 1

wire A

wire B

2. Repeat Step 1 on wire B (Fig. 2).

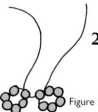

Figure 2

3. String 2 green beads on wire A (Fig. 3).

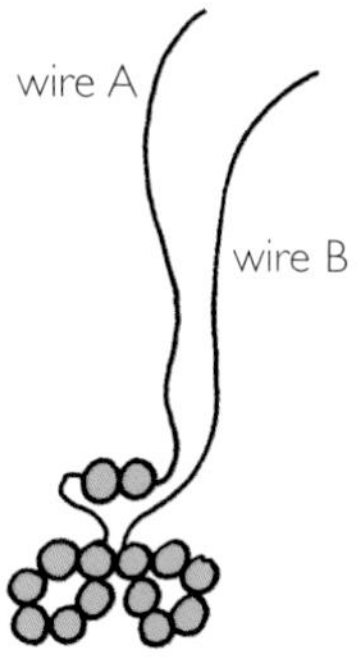

wire A

wire B

Figure 3

4. String wire B back through the same 2 beads in the opposite direction to make row 1 of the tail (Fig. 4).

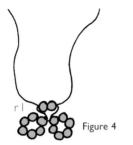

r1

Figure 4

5. To make the rest of the tail and body, add the following rows of beads (Fig. 5):

        row 2: 3 green
        row 3: 4 green
        row 4: 4 green
        row 5: 4 green
        row 6: 4 green
        row 7: 3 light peach
        row 8: 3 red
        row 9: 3 light peach

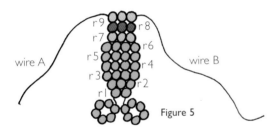

r9   r8
r7
r5   r6
wire A   r3   r4
       r1   r2   wire B

Figure 5

6. To make an arm, add 6 beads to wire A, and string back with wire A through 5 beads, skipping the outermost bead (Fig. 6).

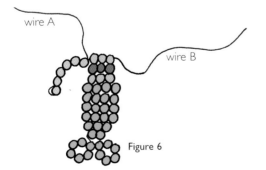

wire A

wire B

Figure 6

7. Repeat Step 6 on wire B to make the second arm (Fig. 7).

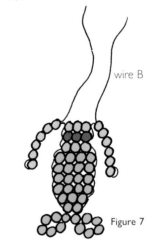

wire B

Figure 7

8. For the head, add the following rows of beads (Fig. 8):

        row 10: 2 light peach
        row 11: 3 light peach
        row 12: 3 light peach

Then bring the wires together and string one red bead (Fig. 8).

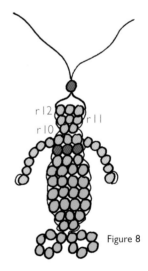

r12   r11
r10

Figure 8

9. For the hair, separate the wires and add 5 black beads to wire A. Then string wire A back through all but the outermost bead. Repeat on wire B to finish hair (Fig. 9).

Figure 9

10. Put the wires together and twist once. Then separate the wires, place a jump ring over them, and twist the wire ends around the jump ring. Trim off the extra wire (Fig. 10).

Figure 10

Now try changing the colors of some beads and the hair style to make a merman.

Merman and Mermaid

Snake

Below are directions for making a coral snake, one of the most poisonous snakes in the world. Want to make a nonpoisonous king snake instead? Easy! Change the pattern a bit: start with a red bead and follow the pattern below with yellow, red, yellow, then black bands.

You Will Need

- jump ring
- 20'' (51 cm) wire
- 19 yellow e beads
- 24 black e beads
- 18 red e beads
- 2 blue e beads
- 11 red seed beads

This pattern is worked from the snake's tail to the head.

1. Center a jump ring on a 20'' wire. We will call one-half wire A and one-half wire B. String wire A through one yellow bead (Fig. 1).

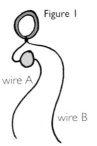

Figure 1

wire A

wire B

2. Loop wire B back through the bead in the opposite direction and pull tight (Fig. 2).

Figure 2

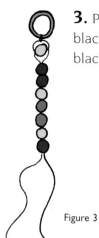

3. Put the wires together and add 2 black, 1 yellow, 2 red, 1 yellow, and 1 black e bead (Fig. 3).

Figure 3

6. Add the following rows of e beads (Fig. 6):

row 2: 2 yellow	row 13: 2 black
row 3: 2 red	row 14: 2 yellow
row 4: 2 red	row 15: 2 red
row 5: 2 yellow	row 16: 2 red
row 6: 2 black	row 17: 2 yellow
row 7: 2 black	row 18: 2 black
row 8: 2 yellow	row 19: 2 black
row 9: 2 red	row 20: 2 yellow
row 10: 2 red	row 21: 2 red
row 11: 2 yellow	row 22: 2 red
row 12: 2 black	row 23: 2 yellow

4. Separate the wires and add 2 e black beads to wire A (Fig. 4).

wire B

wire A

Figure 4

5. String wire B through the 2 black beads from the opposite direction to complete row 1 (Fig. 5).

r1

Figure 5

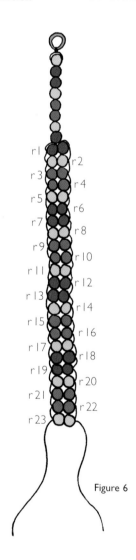

r1
r3
r5
r7
r9
r11
r13
r15
r17
r19
r21
r23

r2
r4
r6
r8
r10
r12
r14
r16
r18
r20
r22

Figure 6

7. To make the head, add the following rows of e beads (Fig. 7):

    row 24: 3 black
    row 25: 1 blue, 1 black, 1 blue
    row 26: 2 black
    row 27: 1 black

Figure 7

8. To make the tongue, put the wires together and string 3 red seed beads (Fig. 8).

9. Separate the wires and add 4 red seed beads to each wire (Fig. 8).

Figure 9

10. Twist the wires around the last of the beads you just strung and trim off the extra wire.

You can also try making a green snake, as shown on page 23.

Figure 8

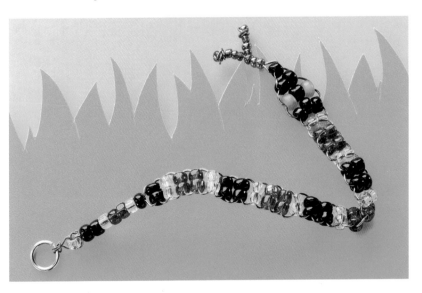

Gecko

Geckos have amazing feet that help them climb walls and even stick upside down! This little guy will be happy to stick with you.

You Will Need

- jump ring
- 26'' (65 cm) wire
- 57 dark green e beads
- 22 light green e beads
- 16 orange e beads
- 2 dark pink e beads

1. Center a jump ring on a 26'' wire. We will call one-half wire A and one-half wire B. Add 2 dark green beads to wire A and push wire B through the beads in the opposite direction to make row 1 (Fig. 1).

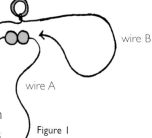

wire B

wire A

Figure 1

2. Pull tight and make sure that there is no extra space between the beads (Fig. 2).

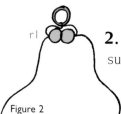

r1

Figure 2

3. To make the head, add the following rows of beads (Fig. 3):

row 2: 3 dark green
row 3: 1 pink, 2 dark green, 1 pink
row 4: 3 dark green
row 5: 2 dark green
row 6: 4 dark green

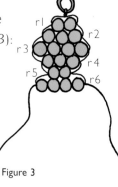

r1

r2

r3

r4

r5

r6

Figure 3

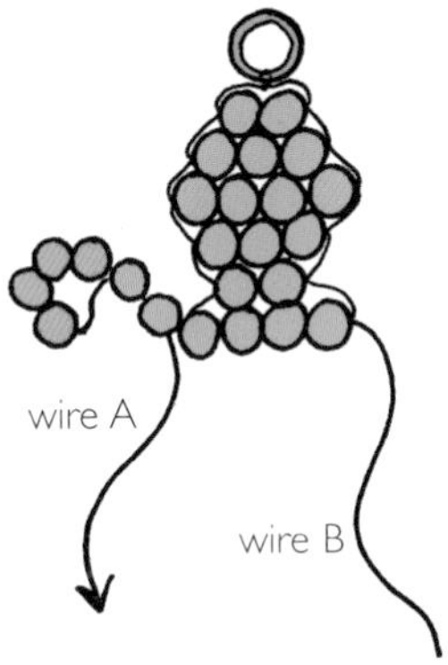

4. To make a front leg and foot, add 2 dark green and then 4 orange beads to wire A. String the same wire back through the first 2 dark green beads as shown (Fig. 4).

wire A

wire B

Figure 4

5. Repeat on the other wire to make another foot (Fig. 5).

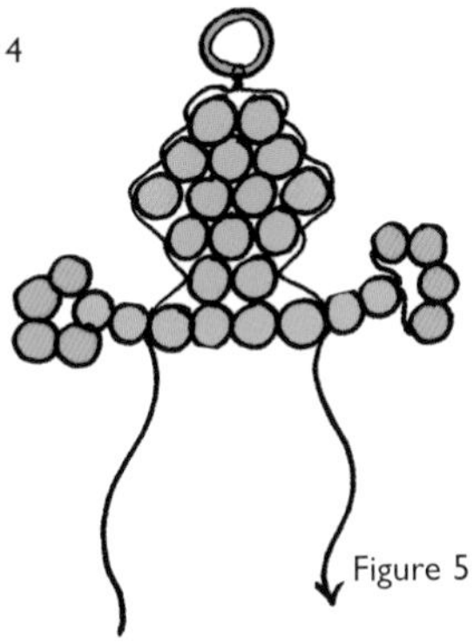

Figure 5

6. To make the body, add the following rows of beads (Fig. 6):

row 7: 1 dark green, 2 light green, 1 dark green
row 8: 1 dark green, 2 light green, 1 dark green
row 9: 1 dark green, 3 light green, 1 dark green
row 10: 1 dark green, 3 light green, 1 dark green
row 11: 1 dark green, 3 light green, 1 dark green
row 12: 1 dark green, 3 light green, 1 dark green
row 13: 1 dark green, 3 light green, 1 dark green
row 14: 1 dark green, 2 light green, 1 dark green

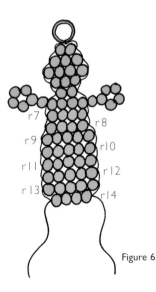

Figure 6

7. To make a back leg, add 2 dark green beads and then 4 orange beads to wire A. String the same wire back through the first 2 dark green beads as shown (Fig. 7). Repeat on the other side to make the second back leg.

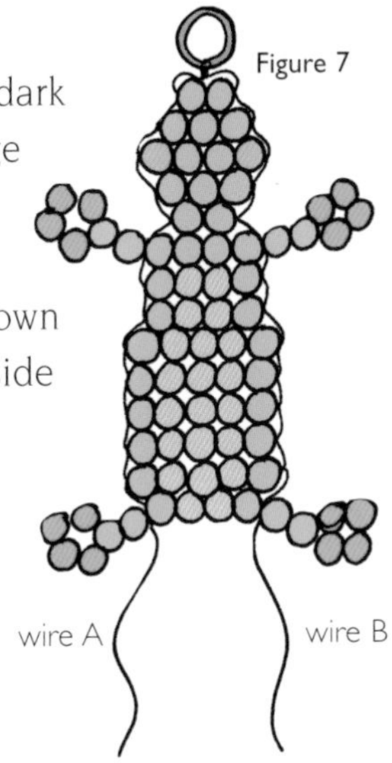

Figure 7

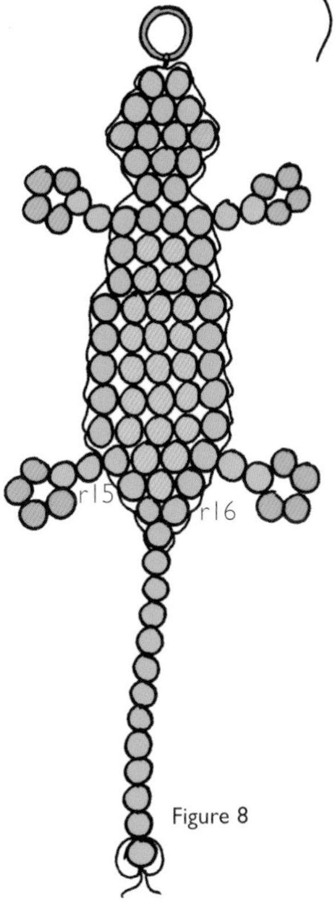

wire A

wire B

Figure 8

8. To start the tail, add the following rows of beads (Fig. 8):

row 15: 1 dark green, 1 light green, 1 dark green
row 16: 2 dark green

Put the wires together and string 13 or more dark green beads (Fig. 8). Separate the wires and string one wire back through the last bead. Then twist the wires together to secure the beads. Trim the excess wire.

Snail

Are you a fan of snails? They are pretty neat animals. They make a slime that allows them to suction up against surfaces. Some can even climb upside down! Make your own snail pal.

You Will Need

- jump ring
- 15" (38 cm) wire
- 12 red e beads
- 8 orange e beads
- 11 green e beads
- 8 green seed beads
- 2 black e beads

1. Center a jump ring on a 15″ wire (Fig. 1). We will call one-half wire A and the other half wire B.

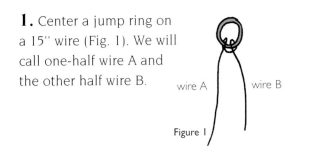

Figure 1

wire A wire B

2. Add the following rows of e beads by stringing on each row with wire A and then stringing back through the row with wire B (Fig. 2), as described on page 8:

row 1: 2 red
row 2: 3 orange
row 3: 4 red
row 4: 5 orange

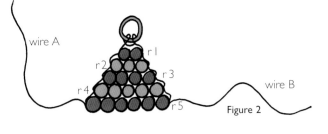

wire A

r1
r2
r3
r4
r5

wire B

Figure 2

3. Add 4 green e beads to wire A and then push wire A back through all but the outermost green bead (Fig. 3).

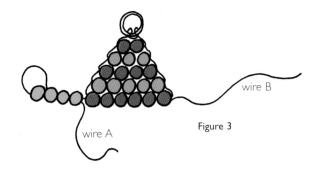

wire B

wire A

Figure 3

4. Continue to push wire A through the red beads on row 5 so both wires end up on the same side (Fig. 4).

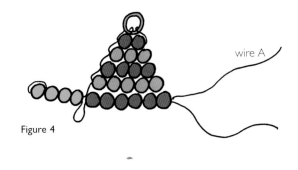

wire A

Figure 4

5. Put the wires together and add 2 green e beads. Then separate the wires and add these 2 rows of e beads (Fig. 5):

row 6: 2 green
row 7: 3 green

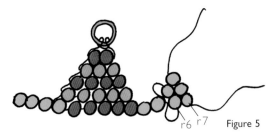

r6 r7 Figure 5

6. To make the snail's tentacles, add 4 green seed beads and 1 black e bead on one wire. Push that wire back through the last (black) bead (Fig. 6). Repeat on the second wire to make the second tentacle. Trim off the excess wire.

Figure 6

Frog

There are over 4500 different types of frog in the world. Try making this blue frog; then change the colors to create a different frog.

You Will Need

- jump ring
- 20" (51 cm) wire
- 2 black beads, either e bead size or 3/0 size for larger eyes
- 67 blue e beads
- 12 green e beads

1. Center a jump ring on the 20" wire. We will call one-half wire A and one-half wire B. String wire A through a blue bead. String wire B through the same blue bead in the opposite direction, as shown (Fig. 1).

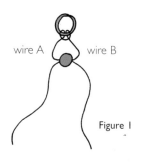

Figure 1

2. Pull tight; then add 2 blue beads and 1 black bead to wire A (Fig. 2).

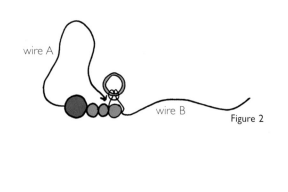

Figure 2

3. String wire A back through the 2 blue beads you just added, as shown in Fig. 3, left (you see the start of stringing in Fig. 2). Repeat on wire B to make the other side (Fig. 3, right). This makes row 1.

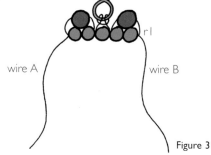

Figure 3

4. Add the following rows of beads, stringing both wires through as shown (Fig. 4):

row 2: 5 blue
row 3: 2 blue
row 4: 5 blue

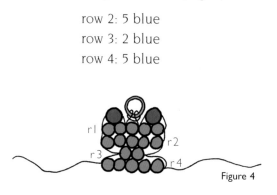

Figure 4

6. Repeat Step 5 on wire B for the other front leg. Then add the next rows of beads (Fig. 6):

row 5: 5 blue
row 6: 6 blue
row 7: 7 blue
row 8: 6 blue

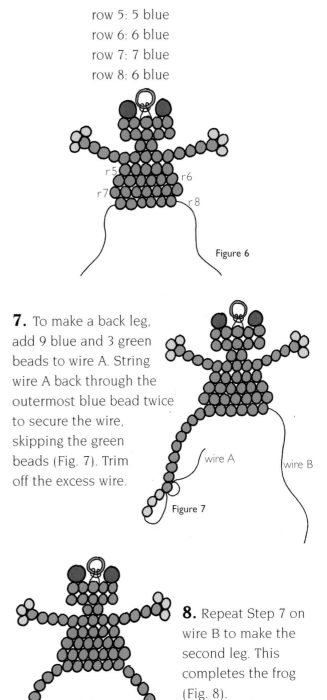

Figure 6

7. To make a back leg, add 9 blue and 3 green beads to wire A. String wire A back through the outermost blue bead twice to secure the wire, skipping the green beads (Fig. 7). Trim off the excess wire.

wire A

wire B

Figure 7

5. To make a front leg, add 4 blue and 3 green beads to wire A. String the same wire back through the 4 blue beads you just added in the opposite direction, skipping the green beads (Fig. 5).

wire B

wire A

Figure 5

8. Repeat Step 7 on wire B to make the second leg. This completes the frog (Fig. 8).

Figure 8

Turtle

Many cultures around the world tell stories about the turtle's tough, strong shell. Stories from India describe the Earth as being held up by a turtle's back. In Native American tales, the world sometimes is described as an island on the back of a turtle. Maybe your turtle won't be able to carry the world on its back, but it might make you feel a little stronger.

1. Center a jump ring on a 26" wire. We will call one-half of it wire A and the other half wire B (Fig. 1).

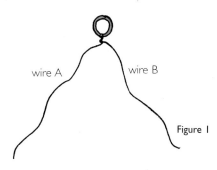

Figure 1

2. Separate the wires and add the following rows of beads (Fig. 2), as described on page 8:

    row 1: 3 light green
    row 2: 4 light green
    row 3: 1 black, 3 light green, 1 black
    row 4: 3 light green

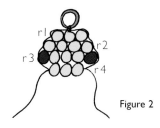

Figure 2

3. Add the following rows of beads (Fig. 3):

    row 5: 7 dark green
    row 6: 1 dark green, 7 medium green,
       1 dark green

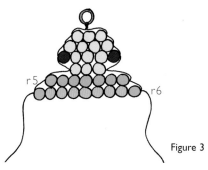

Figure 3

4. To make a front foot, add 6 light green beads to wire A, and string back through the first of these beads with the same wire, as shown (Fig. 4).

5. Repeat on wire B (Fig. 5) for the other front foot.

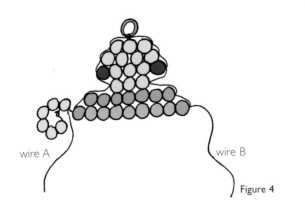

wire A   wire B

Figure 4

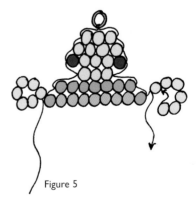

Figure 5

6. Add the following rows of beads (Fig. 6):

   row 7: 1 dark green, 2 medium green, 5 dark
      green, 2 medium green, 1 dark green

   row 8: 1 dark green, 2 medium green, 1 dark
      green, 5 medium green, 1 dark green,
      2 medium green, 1 dark green

   row 9: 1 dark green, 2 medium green, 1 dark
      green, 2 medium green, 1 dark green,
      2 medium green, 1 dark green, 2 medium
      green, 1 dark green

   row 10: 1 dark green, 2 medium green,
      1 dark green, 5 medium green, 1 dark
      green, 2 medium green, 1 dark green

   row 11: 1 dark green, 2 medium green, 5 dark
      green, 2 medium green, 1 dark green

   row 12: 1 dark green, 7 medium green,
      1 dark green

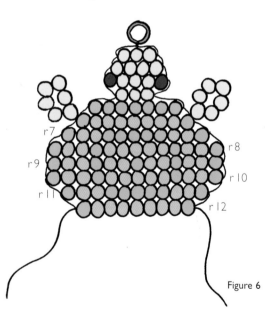

Figure 6

7. For the first back foot, add 6 light green beads to wire A and string back through the first of the 6 beads just added as shown (Fig. 7). Repeat on wire B for the second back foot.

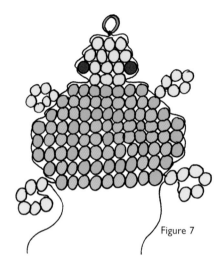

Figure 7

8. Add these rows of beads (Fig. 8):

   row 13: 7 dark green
   row 14: 2 light green
   row 15: 1 light green

Twist the ends of the wires together and trim off the extra wire.

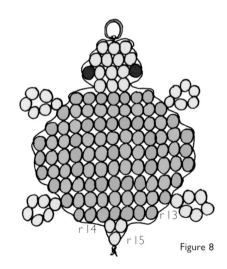

Figure 8

Ladybug

Did you know that the ladybug is a type of beetle? It's one of the most loved insects, especially beloved by farmers, who often depend on ladybugs to eat garden pests. Make your own ladybug; maybe it will keep pests away.

You Will Need

- 20" (51 cm) wire
- 3" (7.5 cm) wire
- jump ring
- 60 red e beads
- 18 green e beads
- 20 black e beads

This pattern is worked from the bottom up.

1. String row 1 on the 20" wire at the center: 2 red, 1 black, 2 red beads (Fig. 1). One-half of the wire is wire A and the other half is called wire B.

wire A   wire B

r1

Figure 1

2. On wire A, add these beads to make row 2: 4 red, 1 black, 2 red, 1 black, 1 red (Fig. 2). String back through them in the opposite direction with wire B.

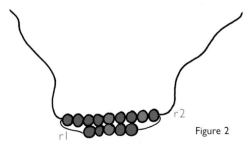

r2

r1

Figure 2

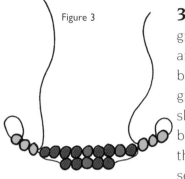

Figure 3

3. To make a leg, add 3 green beads to one wire, and string the same wire back through the first 2 green beads added, skipping the outermost bead (Fig. 3). Repeat on the other wire to make a second leg.

4. Add the following rows of beads (Fig. 4):

> row 3: 2 red, 1 black, 1 red, 1 black, 4 red
> row 4: 5 red, 1 black, 5 red

To make the next pair of legs (Fig. 4), add 3 green beads to one wire, stringing the same wire back through the first 2 green beads added, skipping the outermost bead. Repeat on the other wire.

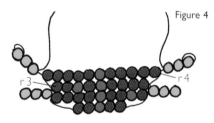

Figure 4

5. Add the following rows of beads (Fig. 5):

> row 5: 5 red, 1 black, 2 red, 1 black, 2 red
> row 6: 5 red, 1 black, 5 red

To make the last pair of legs, add 3 green beads to one wire, stringing the same wire back through the first 2 green beads added, skipping the outermost bead. Repeat on the other wire.

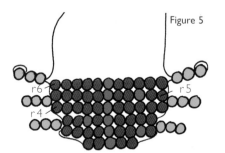

Figure 5

6. Add the following rows of beads (Fig. 6):

> row 7: 1 red, 1 black, 2 red, 1 black, 4 red
> row 8: 3 red, 1 black, 2 red, 1 black
> row 9: 4 black
> row 10: 3 black

String a new 3" wire through row 10 as shown.

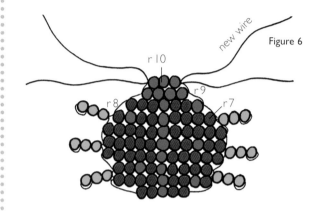

Figure 6

7. Twist the two ends of the new wire together above the center of row 10. Then twist it around a jump ring to secure it. Trim off the excess wire (Fig. 7). Trim back the two remaining wires until they are each 1" (2.5 cm) long. Curl them to make antennae.

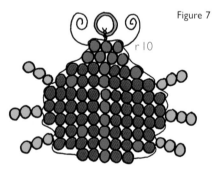

Figure 7

Spider

Are spiders insects? No! All insects have six legs. Spiders have eight. Make sure to give your spider the right number of legs.

1. Center 3 black e beads on the 10" wire. We will call one end wire A and one end wire B. String wire B back through the row of beads as shown to make row 1 (Fig. 1).

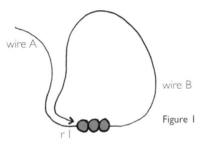

wire A

wire B

Figure 1

r 1

2. In the same way, add the following rows of e beads (Fig. 2):

> row 2: 5 black
> row 3: 5 black
> row 4: 3 black

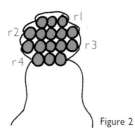

Figure 2

3. String wire A back through the last row of beads (Fig. 3).

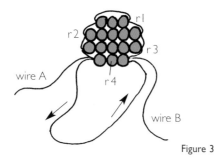

Figure 3

4. String one of the 5" pieces of wire, wire C, through row 1. String another 5" wire, wire D, through row 2. String another 5" wire, wire E, through row 3 (Fig. 4).

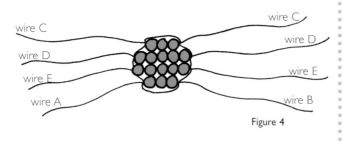

Figure 4

5. Add 11 black seed beads to each wire end (Fig. 5), including wire A and wire B, stringing each wire back through the last bead of its row to secure the beads. Trim off all the extra wire.

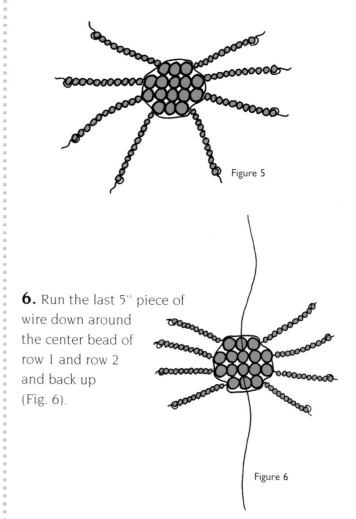

Figure 5

6. Run the last 5" piece of wire down around the center bead of row 1 and row 2 and back up (Fig. 6).

Figure 6

7. Put both wire ends together, and then twist them around a jump ring several times. Trim off the extra wire (Fig. 7).

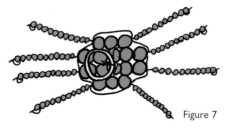

Figure 7

Bee

In order to communicate with each other, bees do a dance. If flowers are close by, the bee moves in circles. If flowers are far away, the bee waggles its body and does figure-eights. Make your own bee and try your own waggle dance!

You Will Need

- 15" (38 cm) wire
- 3" (7.5 cm) wire
- jump ring
- 12 black e beads
- 50 gold seed beads
- 16 yellow e beads

This pattern is worked from the bottom up.

1. String 3 yellow beads onto a 15" wire and center them to make row 1 (Fig. 1). One end of the wire is called wire A. One end is wire B. Run wire B back through the yellow beads you just added and pull tight.

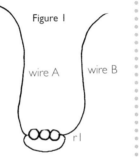

Figure 1

wire A   wire B

r1

2. Add the following rows of e beads, stringing them on one wire end and back through them with the other wire end (Fig. 2):

row 2: 5 black
row 3: 6 yellow
row 4: 5 black
row 5: 3 yellow

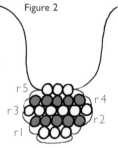

Figure 2

r5   r4
r3   r2
r1

3. For a wing, string 24 gold seed beads onto wire A, and then string the same wire back through the yellow beads of row 5 (Fig. 3).

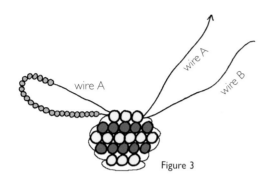

Figure 3

4. To make the second wing, repeat Step 3 on wire B (Fig. 4).

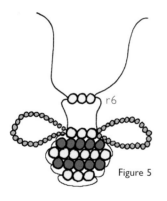

Figure 4

5. Next, add row 6, 3 yellow e beads (Fig. 5).

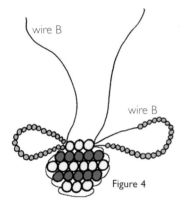

Figure 5

6. String on these e beads to make row 7: 1 black, 1 yellow, 1 black (Fig. 6).

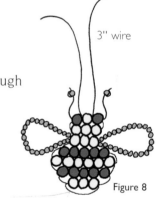

Figure 6

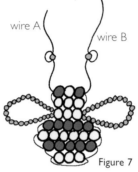

Figure 7

7. For an antenna, add one gold seed bead to wire A about ½" (1 cm) up the wire (Fig. 7). String the same wire back through the gold bead to secure it in place, or twist the wire around itself. Trim off the extra wire. Repeat on wire B for the second antenna.

8. String the 3" wire through the yellow center bead in row 7 (Fig. 8).

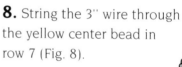

Figure 8

9. Twist the wire ends together, and then twist them around a jump ring (Fig. 9). Trim off the extra wire.

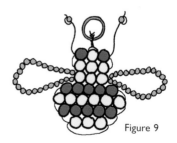

Figure 9

Baby Fish

Fish are found all over the Earth, in both freshwater and salt water. Some live alone and some live in groups called schools. They pay attention in school, but they don't get much homework.

This figure is worked from the nose of the fish back towards the tail. We'll make the orange fish.

1. Center the jump ring on the 10" wire (Fig. 1).

Figure 1

2. Add the following rows of beads by stringing each row on one wire end and then stringing the other wire end back through the same beads. See page 8 for general instructions on making rows (Fig. 2):

row 1: 2 orange
row 2: 1 orange, 1 black, 2 orange
row 3: 5 orange
row 4: 5 orange
row 5: 5 orange
row 6: 4 orange
row 7: 2 orange
row 8: 3 orange
row 9: 5 orange

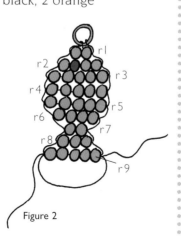

Figure 2

Loop one wire end back through row 9 to secure the beads; pull tight.

3. Put the wire ends together on one side and twist them together a few times. Trim off the extra wire (Fig. 3).

Once you have made one baby fish, change the colors and make yourself a school of baby fish.

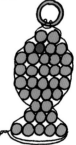

Figure 3

Jellyfish

Is a jellyfish a fish? No! In fact, many people now call the jellyfish the "sea jelly" to avoid confusion. Try making your own sea jelly.

1. Center 5 dark blue e beads on the 10" wire. One-half is wire A and one-half is wire B. String wire B back through the beads as shown.

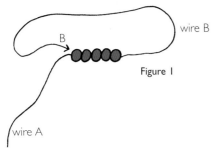

Figure 1

You Will Need

- jump ring
- 10" (25 cm) wire
- two 5" (12.5 cm) wires
- 3" (7.5 cm) wire
- 19 light blue e beads
- 16 dark blue e beads
- 90 light blue seed beads

2. Pull tight to make row 1 (Fig. 2).

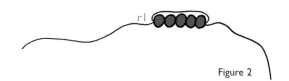

Figure 2

3. Add the following rows of e beads in the same way (Fig. 3):

> row 2: 1 dark blue, 6 light blue, 1 dark blue
> row 3: 1 dark blue, 7 light blue, 1 dark blue
> row 4: 1 dark blue, 6 light blue, 1 dark blue
> row 5: 5 dark blue

Then loop one wire back through the last row of beads (Fig. 3) and pull tight.

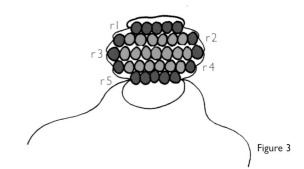

Figure 3

4. To make a tentacle, add 15 light blue seed beads to wire A. Loop wire A back through the last bead to secure it (Fig. 4). Trim off the extra wire. Repeat on wire B to make another tentacle.

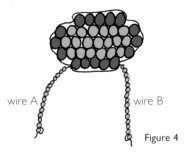

wire A   wire B

Figure 4

5. On row 3, string through and center one of the 5" wires, which we'll call wire C (Fig. 5). String the other 5" wire (wire D) through row 1.

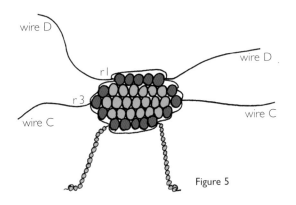

wire D

wire D

r 1

r 3

wire C   wire C

Figure 5

6. Make a tentacle on each end of wire C and on each end of wire D as you did in Step 4 (Fig. 6).

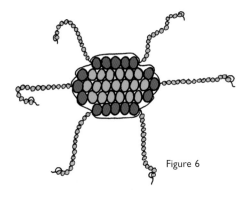

Figure 6

7. String the 3" wire through bead 5 of row 3 (Fig. 7).

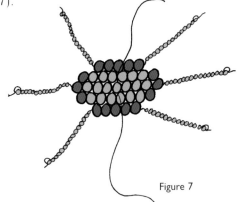

Figure 7

8. Put the wire ends together close to the beads, twist once, and then twist the wires around a jump ring. Trim off the extra wire (Fig. 8).

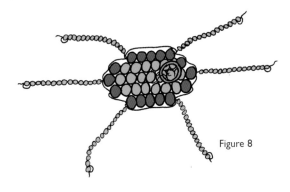

Figure 8

9. Finally, use your thumb to push up on the center of the body from below so that your jellyfish has a dome shape (Fig. 9).

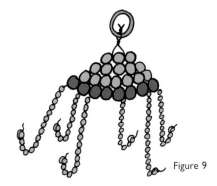

Figure 9

Lobster

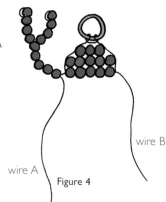

Most live lobsters are bluish green. Rare ones are sometimes orange, yellow, or blue. When they are cooked, they turn red. Try making this red cooked lobster and then change the red beads to another color of your choice to make a live lobster.

You Will Need

- jump ring
- 24" (61 cm) wire
- 93 red e beads
- 2 black e beads

1. Center a jump ring on the wire. We will call one-half wire A and one-half wire B. To start the head, string 3 red beads onto wire A, and then string wire B through the same beads in the opposite direction to make row 1 (Fig. 1).

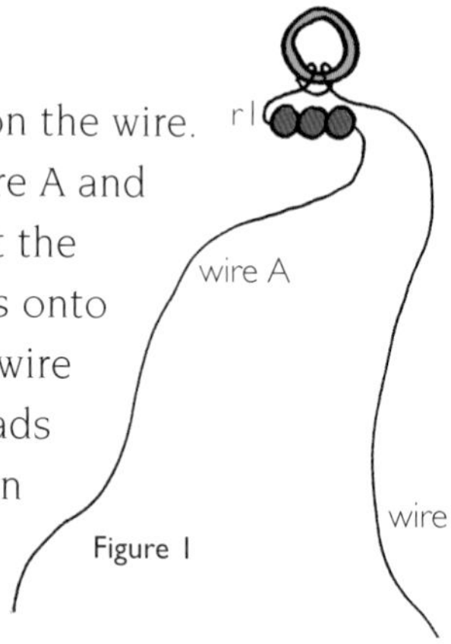

wire A

wire B

Figure 1

2. In the same way, add 2 more rows of beads (Fig. 2):

    row 2: 1 red, 1 black, 1 red, 1 black, 1 red
    row 3: 5 red

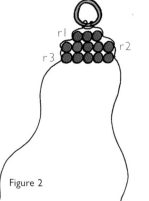

Figure 2

3. To make a claw, string 9 red beads onto wire A. Then string wire A back through beads 8, 7, and 6 (skipping 9, the outermost), as shown (Fig. 3).

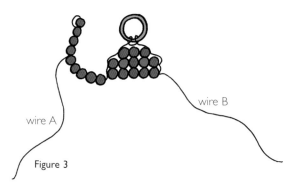

wire A

wire B

Figure 3

4. Add 4 more red beads to wire A. Then string wire A back towards the head through all 8 beads in a straight line, except the outermost bead (Fig. 4).

wire A

wire B

Figure 4

5. Repeat steps 3 and 4 on wire B to make a second claw (Fig. 5). Then add the following rows of beads to continue the body:

row 4: 4 red
row 5: 5 red
row 6: 5 red

Add 3 red beads to wire A and string back through the first 2 you added, skipping the outermost bead (Fig. 5).

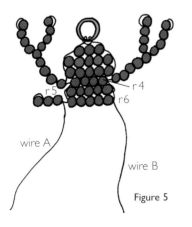

r 5
r 4
r 6

wire A

wire B

Figure 5

6. In the same way, add 3 red beads to wire B, and string back through the first 2 beads you added (Fig. 6).

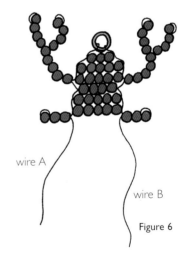

wire A

wire B

Figure 6

7. Add row 7 (Fig. 7), 5 red beads.

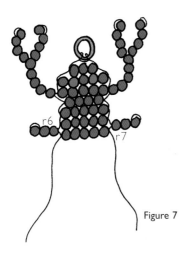

Figure 7

8. Add row 8, 5 red beads (Fig. 8). Then add 3 red beads to wire A and string back through the first 2 of these 3 beads, skipping the outermost bead. Repeat on wire B.

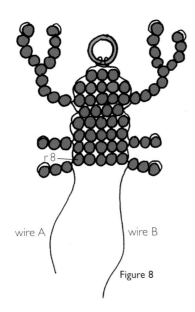

wire A   wire B

Figure 8

9. Add the following rows of beads (Fig. 9):

row 9: 4 red
row 10: 3 red
row 11: 2 red
row 12: 4 red
row 13: 7 red

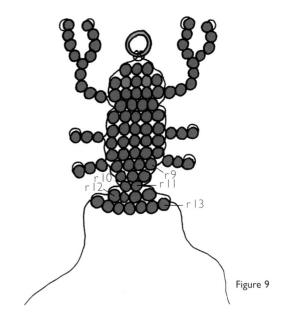

Figure 9

10. String wire A back through all but the outermost bead in row 13 (Fig. 10). Twist the wires together and trim off the excess wire.

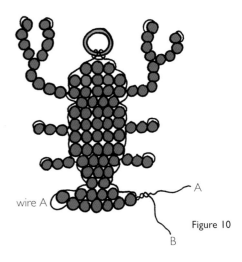

wire A

Figure 10

Squid

Squid are relatives of octopuses. Neither animal has bones. Squid live in oceans all over the world. Small squid are quite common. The giant squid, as big as a whale, lurks in the deep ocean and is hardly ever seen. Make this small squid so it can swim on your backpack.

You Will Need

- jump ring
- 10'' (25 cm) wire
- four 6'' (14 cm) wires
- 24 red e beads
- 31 orange e beads
- 2 black e beads
- 108 orange seed beads

1. Center a jump ring on the 10″ wire. We will call one-half wire A and one-half wire B. Then string on the following rows of e beads (Fig. 1). See page 8 for general instructions on stringing on rows of beads:

row 1: 1 orange
row 2: 2 orange
row 3: 1 orange, 1 red, 1 orange
row 4: 1 orange, 2 red, 1 orange
row 5: 1 orange, 3 red, 1 orange
row 6: 1 orange, 4 red, 1 orange
row 7: 1 orange, 5 red, 1 orange
row 8: 1 orange, 1 red, 1 black, 2 red, 1 black,
    1 red, 1 orange
row 9: 1 orange, 5 red, 1 orange
row 10: 6 orange

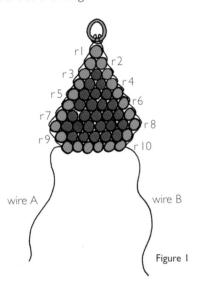

Figure 1

2. To make a tentacle, add 20 orange seed beads to wire A, and string wire A back through the last bead to secure the beads (Fig. 2). Trim off the extra of wire A. Make another tentacle on wire B in the same way but string on only 16 beads.

Figure 2

3. String one of the 6″ wires through the second bead of row 10 and another 6″ wire through the fifth bead of row 10. We'll call these wire ends C, D, E, and F (Fig. 3).

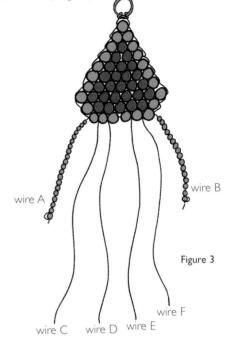

wire A

wire B

wire C   wire D wire E

wire F

Figure 3

4. Add 16 orange seed beads to wire end C, stringing the wire back through the last bead to secure the beads. Trim off the extra wire. Add 20 orange seed beads to wire end D, add 16 orange seed beads to wire end E, and add 20 orange seed beads to wire end F in the same manner (Fig. 4), securing the beads and trimming off the extra wire to make 6 tentacles in all.

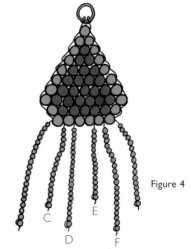

C

E

D

F

Figure 4

5. String one of the remaining 6" wires (wire G) so it goes in through the wire on the edge between rows 2 and 3 and comes out through the wire on the edge between rows 4 and 5 as shown (Fig. 5). String the other wire (wire H) on the other side of the squid body in the same way, as shown (Fig. 5).

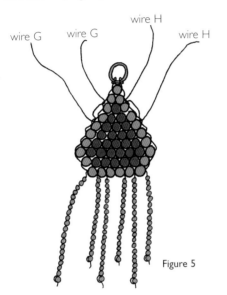

Figure 5

6. Add 4 orange e beads to one end of wire G and string the other end of wire G through the 4 beads in the opposite direction (Fig. 6). Repeat on wire H.

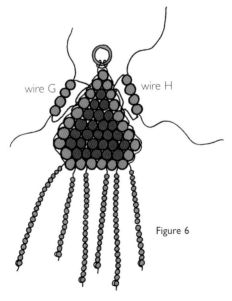

Figure 6

7. String both ends of wire G back through all the orange beads in the loop, put the wire ends of G together, and twist them together (Fig. 7). Trim off the extra wire and tuck the ends in. Repeat with wire H.

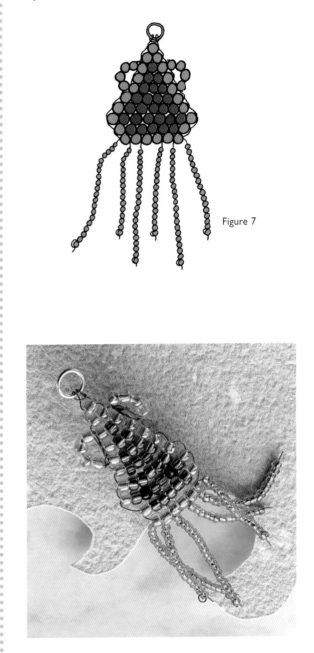

Figure 7

Seahorse

Did you know that seahorses are fish? Ancient Egyptians thought that sea-horses could help them find their way up the Nile River. Keep your seahorse with you. Maybe it will keep you from getting lost!

You Will Need

- jump ring
- 30'' (76 cm) wire
- 3'' (7.5 cm) wire
- 8'' (20 cm) wire (if you want to add fins)
- 92 dark green e beads
- 24 light green e beads
- 1 black e bead

We'll start with the snout. The first 4 rows will run vertically.

1. String 2 dark green beads onto the center of the 30'' wire. String one end of the wire back through the beads and pull tight so that the beads are secured (Fig. 1). One-half is wire A and one-half is wire B.

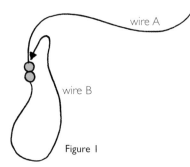

Figure 1

2. Put wires A and B together and string on 2 dark green beads (Fig. 2). Separate the two wires and string 1 dark green bead on wire A (Fig. 2). String wire B through this last dark green bead in the opposite direction.

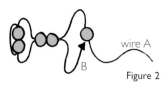

Figure 2

3. String 2 dark green beads on wire A (Fig. 3). String wire B back through the beads in the opposite direction to make row 1.

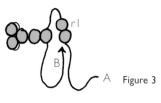

Figure 3

4. String 3 beads on wire A: 1 dark green, 1 black, and 1 dark green. String wire B back through the beads to make row 2 (Fig. 4).

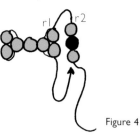

Figure 4

5. Make row 3, 4 dark green beads. Then string 5 beads on wire A: 1 light green bead, then 4 dark green beads to make row 4 (Fig. 5).

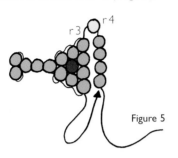

Figure 5

6. String wire B back through the 4 dark green beads but not through the last light green bead of row 4 (Fig. 6).

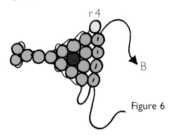

Figure 6

7. Add one light green bead to wire B. Loop wire B back through the third bead in row 4 as shown (Fig. 7).

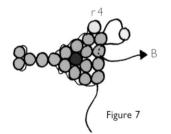

Figure 7

8. String another light green bead on wire B, and string wire B through the bottom dark green bead of row 4 (Fig. 8).

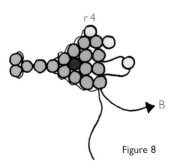

Figure 8

9. Bring both wires together and string 6 dark green beads on both together. Separate the wires and add 1 light green and 1 dark green bead to wire A. String wire B back through these 2 beads to make row 5 (Fig. 9).

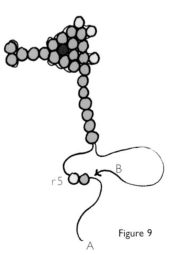

Figure 9

10. Add the following rows of beads (Fig. 10), measuring them across:

row 6: 1 light green, 2 dark green
row 7: 2 light green, 3 dark green

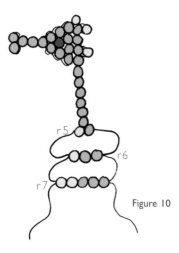

Figure 10

11. Add the following rows of beads (Fig. 11), still working across:

row 8: 3 light green, 4 dark green
row 9: 4 light green, 4 dark green
row 10: 4 light green, 4 dark green
row 11: 3 light green, 3 dark green
row 12: 2 light green, 3 dark green
row 13: 1 light green, 2 dark green
row 14: 2 dark green

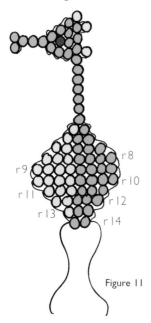

Figure 11

12. For the tail, put both wire ends together and string on 21 dark green beads. After that, separate the wires and loop each one back through the last bead. Pull tight and trim the extra wire (Fig. 12).

Figure 12

13. Curl the tail with your fingers (Fig. 13). String the 3" wire through the light green bead at the top of the seahorse's head, as shown.

Figure 13

14. Bring the ends of the wire together and twist once. Now add your jump ring and twist 2 more times. Trim off the extra wire (Fig. 14).

Congratulations! You made a seahorse. You can stop here if you like, but if you want to add fins to your seahorse, follow the next set of directions.

Figure 14

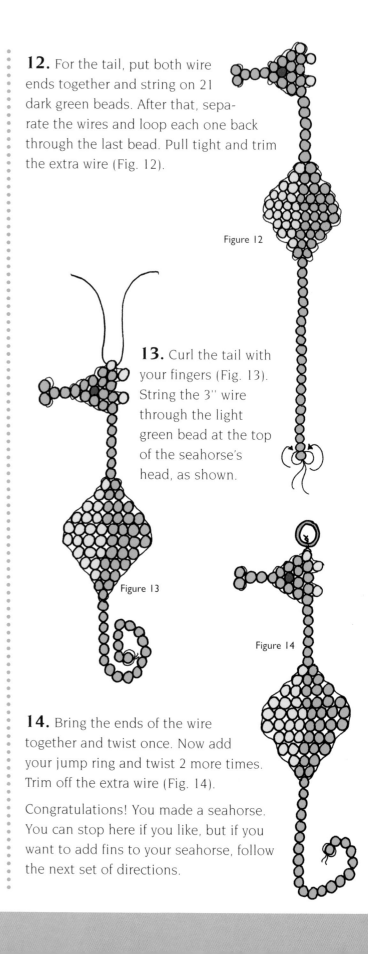

15. For the fin, we make vertical rows. String 5 dark green beads onto the center of the 8'' wire to make row A. Run one end of the wire around and through all the beads again (Fig. 15).

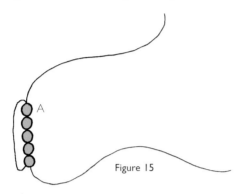

Figure 15

16. Add 2 more rows of beads (Fig. 16):

> row B: 3 dark green
> row C: 2 dark green

Put the wires together and twist the wires together twice (don't trim yet).

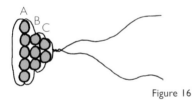

Figure 16

17. Separate the wires and pass their ends through the seahorse's body, one wire end between rows 8 and 9 and the other end between rows 10 and 11, as shown (Fig. 17). Pull the fin and the wires close to the body from the other side.

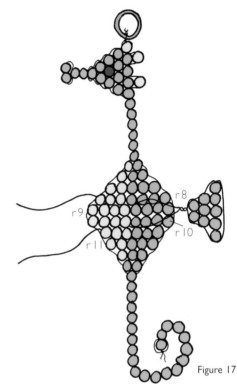

Figure 17

18. Flip the body over and put the wires together, and tightly twist them together twice. Then make the second fin by adding vertical rows of beads (Fig. 18):

> row D: 2 dark green
> row E: 3 dark green
> row F: 5 dark green

Bring the ends of the wires together, and twist once close to the fin to secure. Trim off the extra wire, turning the ends in so they don't stick out.

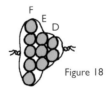

Figure 18

Octopus

The octopus is one of the smartest animals in the ocean. It is quick to learn. Octopuses sometimes learn things from other octopuses. See if your octopus helps you to learn things.

You Will Need*

- jump ring
- large bead, about 1" (2.5 cm) in diameter
- 48" (122 cm) wire
- 25" (63 cm) wires, 5 to 6 pieces
- light blue e beads
- 2 black beads, a bit larger than e beads

*Because the large bead that you find might not be exactly 1" (2.5 cm) diameter, the amount of wire and the number of beads needed may vary slightly from what is listed here.

1. Center a jump ring on the 48" wire. One-half is wire A. The other half is wire B. String both ends through the large bead (Fig. 1).

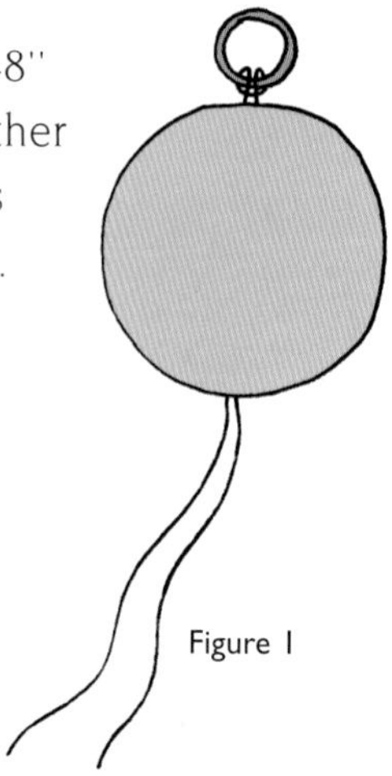

Figure 1

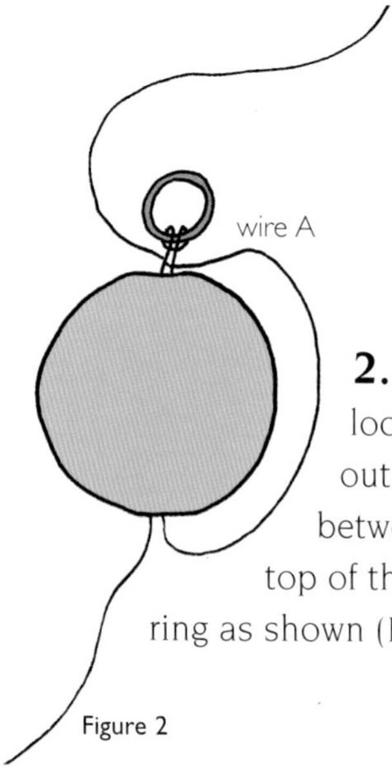

wire A

2. Separate the wires and loop wire A up along the outside of the big bead and between the two wires at the top of the bead under the jump ring as shown (Fig. 2).

Figure 2

3. Add 1 blue bead to wire B. String wire B back through this bead as shown (Fig. 3).

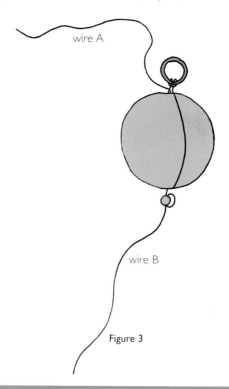

wire A

wire B

Figure 3

4. Add 7 more blue beads, 1 big black bead, and 2 blue beads to wire B, stringing wire B back through the outermost blue bead (Fig. 4).

wire A

wire B

Figure 4

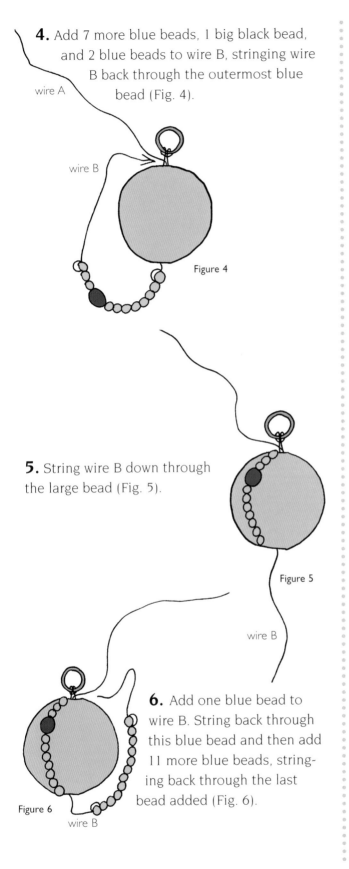

5. String wire B down through the large bead (Fig. 5).

Figure 5

wire B

6. Add one blue bead to wire B. String back through this blue bead and then add 11 more blue beads, stringing back through the last bead added (Fig. 6).

Figure 6

wire B

7. String back down through the large bead with wire B (Fig. 7).

wire B

wire B

Figure 7

8. Make an octopus tentacle by adding one blue bead to wire B, stringing back through the blue bead, and adding 29 more blue beads. Then string through the last blue bead to secure it (Fig. 8). Trim off the extra wire.

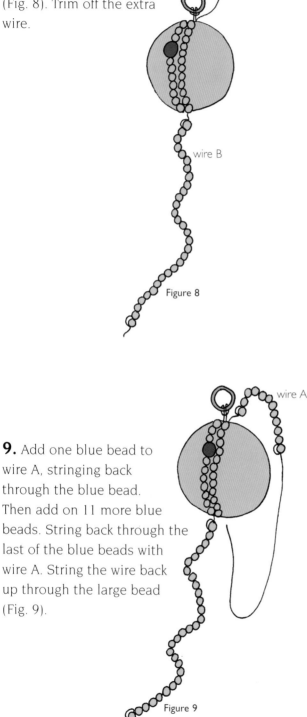

wire B

Figure 8

9. Add one blue bead to wire A, stringing back through the blue bead. Then add on 11 more blue beads. String back through the last of the blue beads with wire A. String the wire back up through the large bead (Fig. 9).

wire A

Figure 9

10. Add 1 blue bead to wire A. String the wire back through this blue bead. Add 2 more blue beads, 1 big black bead, and 7 blue beads to wire A and loop the wire back through the last blue bead. Bring wire A back down along the outside of the large bead and twist it around the first tentacle (Fig. 10).

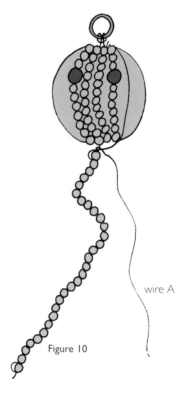

wire A

Figure 10

11. Make a second octopus tentacle by adding one blue bead to wire A and stringing back through the blue bead. Then add 29 more beads and string back through the last blue bead. Trim off the extra wire (Fig. 11).

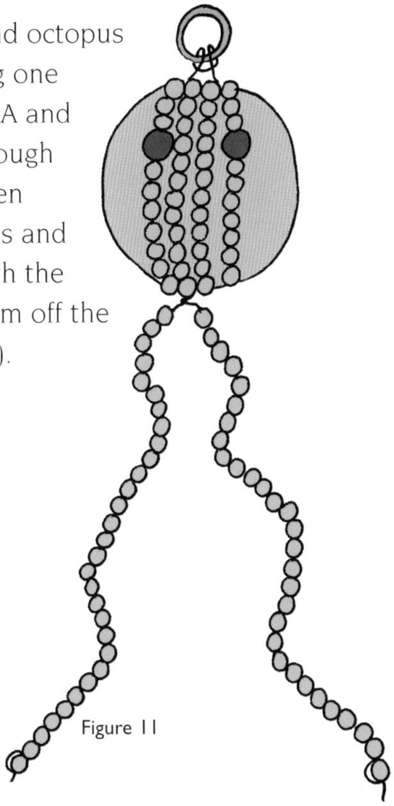

Figure 11

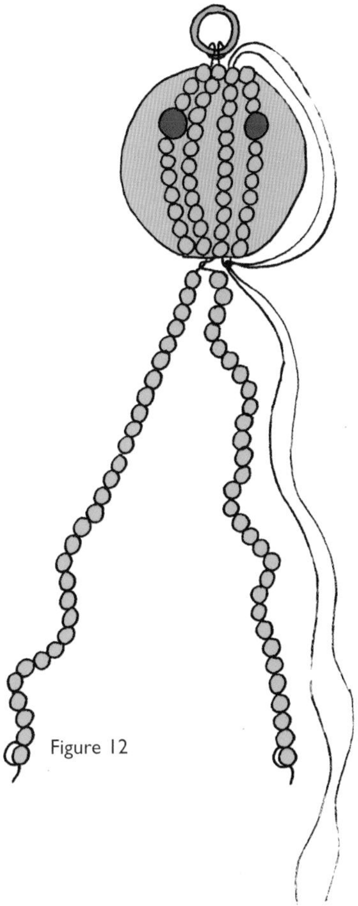

12. Take a piece of 25'' wire and fold it in half. String the folded wire down through the big bead until a loop shows at the bottom of the bead. Now you have two ends of wire and one end that is a loop. Bring the wire ends around the large bead and through the loop of the looped end (Fig. 12).

Figure 12

13. Separate the wires. One is wire C and one is wire D. Add 1 blue bead to wire C, stringing back through this blue bead. Then add 11 more blue beads, stringing back through the last bead. Bring wire C up and string it down through the large bead (Fig. 13). Make a tentacle on the rest of the wire.

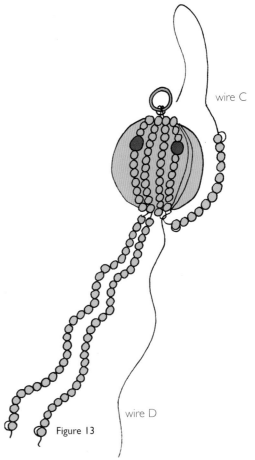

wire C

wire D

Figure 13

14. Repeat step 13 on wire D.

15. Add two more 25'' wires and keep adding beads until the face of the large bead is covered with blue bead rows and there are 8 tentacles.

Octopuses can change color. Try making an octopus with different colored beads.

Penguin

Penguins live in Antarctica. Although they are birds, they don't fly. Penguins have a layer of fat under their skin, which helps them stay warm. Make a penguin to keep you company on cold days.

You Will Need

- jump ring
- 24" (61 cm) wire
- 6" (14 cm) wire
- 81 black e beads
- 64 white e beads
- 21 orange e beads
- 2 light blue e beads

The beak is a separate beaded flap. It is made on a separate wire.

1. Center a jump ring on the 24" wire. We will call one-half wire A and one-half wire B. String 6 black beads on wire A. String wire B through the beads in the opposite direction to make row 1 (Fig. 1).

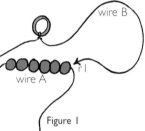

Figure 1

2. Add the following rows of beads in the same way (Fig. 2):

> row 2: 2 black, 1 blue, 2 black, 1 blue, 2 black
> row 3: 3 black, 4 orange, 3 black

Then string the 6" wire through the orange beads in row 3.

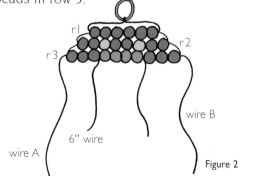

Figure 2

3. To make the beak, add 2 rows of beads on the 6" wire (Fig. 3):

> row A: 2 orange
> row B: 1 orange

Then put the wires together, twist them a few times to secure, and trim off the extra part of the 6" wire.

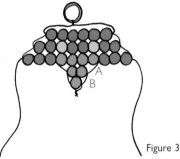

Figure 3

4. Add row 4, 10 black beads, on wire A and string wire B back through the beads. To make a wing, add 15 black beads to wire A, stringing wire A back through the first bead (Fig. 4). Repeat on wire B to make the second wing.

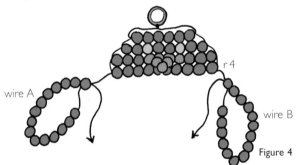

wire A

r 4

wire B

Figure 4

5. String 1 black, 7 white, and 1 black bead on wire A. Then string wire B through the beads in the opposite direction to make row 5 (Fig. 5).

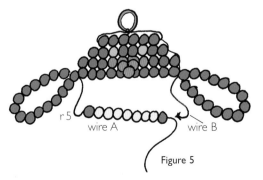

r 5

wire A   wire B

Figure 5

6. Add the following rows of beads (Fig. 6):

> row 6: 1 black, 9 white, 1 black
> row 7: 1 black, 9 white, 1 black
> row 8: 1 black, 10 white, 1 black
> row 9: 1 black, 11 white, 1 black
> row 10: 1 black, 10 white, 1 black
> row 11: 1 black, 8 white, 1 black
> row 12: 9 black

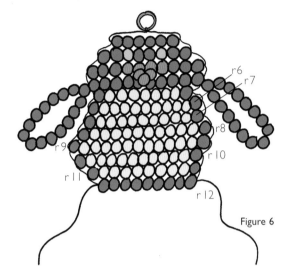

r 6
r 7
r 8
r 9
r 10
r 11
r 12

Figure 6

7. To make a foot, add 7 orange beads to wire A. String the same wire back through the first orange bead twice (Fig. 7); then trim off the extra wire. Make the second foot on wire B the same way. Your penguin is now done.

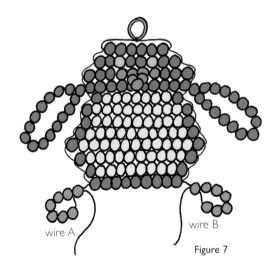

wire A   wire B

Figure 7

Bat

Bats get a bad rap! To some people, bats are scary and spooky. Bats are important animals. They pollinate flowers and eat insects. In China, bats are loved and respected. Bats are said to bring happiness and good luck. Make your own bat and see if it brings good luck to you!

This pattern is worked in the center first, from the bottom up. Then the wings are added.

You Will Need

- jump ring
- three 10'' (25 cm) wires
- 97 black e beads
- 2 blue e beads

1. String 5 beads, centered, onto a 10'' wire. One-half of the wire is called wire A and one-half is wire B. String one end of the wire through the beads again, as shown in Fig. 1. This will be row 1.

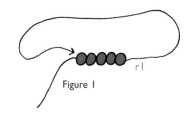

Figure 1

2. Then string on the following rows of beads (Fig. 2):

> row 2: 7 black
> row 3: 7 black
> row 4: 1 black, 1 blue, 2 black, 1 blue,
>   1 black

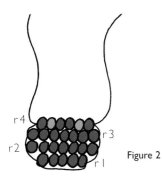

Figure 2

3. To make an ear, string 3 black beads on wire A, stringing the wire back as shown through all 3 beads (Fig. 3).

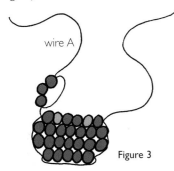

wire A

Figure 3

4. String wire A back through the third bead of row 4 (Fig. 4). Repeat Step 3 with wire B. Then string wire B back through the fourth bead of row 4 (Fig. 4).

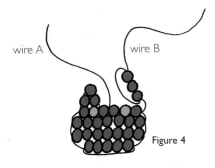

wire A   wire B

Figure 4

5. Twist the 2 wires together, and then twist around a jump ring (Fig. 5). Trim off excess wire.

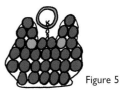

Figure 5

6. To start the wings, run a 10" wire through row 2 and another 10" wire through row 3, as shown (Fig. 6). We will call the ends of the wires C, D, E, and F.

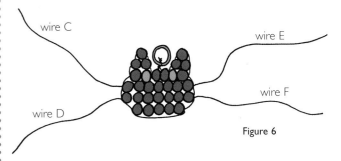

wire C   wire E

wire D   wire F

Figure 6

7. String 4 black beads onto wire C, and run wire D back through the beads you just added in the opposite direction to make row 5 (Fig. 7), which is vertical.

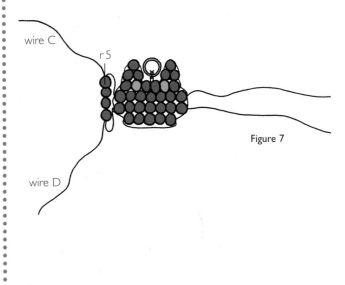

wire C   r5

wire D

Figure 7

8. Add the following vertical rows of beads (Fig. 8) the same way, on wires C and D:

> row 6: 5 black
> row 7: 7 black
> row 8: 5 black
> row 9: 6 black
> row 10: 4 black
> row 11: 3 black

Twist the ends of wires C and D together a few times; then trim off the extra wire.

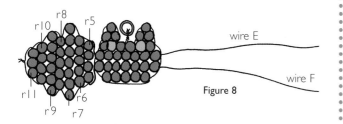

Figure 8

9. Repeat all of steps 7 and 8 on the other side of the bat, but use wires E and F instead, to make the second wing (Fig. 9).

Figure 9

Cat

Cats come in many colors and shapes. Cats were revered as gods in ancient Egypt. They are independent, but often make very good friends. Here is a beaded cat who always will be willing to travel with you.

You Will Need
- jump ring
- 36" (91 cm) wire
- two 1" (2.5 cm) pieces of wire
- two 5" (12.5 cm) pieces of wire
- 215 black e beads
- 1 red e bead
- 6 pink or purple e beads
- 2 clear e beads

1. String 2 black, 1 red, and 2 black beads onto the center of the 36" wire. One-half of this wire is wire A and one-half is wire B. String the two 1" lengths of wire through the red bead for whiskers (Fig. 1).

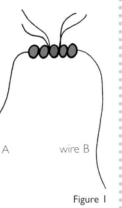

wire A   wire B

Figure 1

2. Add the following rows of beads on wire A, stringing back through them with wire B (Fig. 2). See general instructions for making rows on page 8:

> row 2: 2 black, 1 clear, 3 black,
> 1 clear, 2 black
> row 3: 10 black
> row 4: 12 black

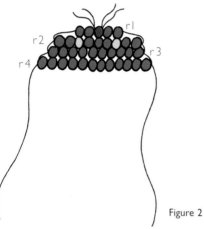

Figure 2

3. String one 5" wire (wire C) through beads 2, 3, 4, and 5 of row 4 (Fig. 3). String the other 5" wire (wire D) through beads 8, 9, 10, and 11 of row 4.

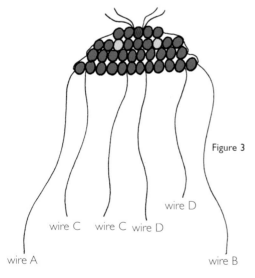

Figure 3

4. To make an ear, add the following rows of beads to wire C (Fig. 4):

> row A: 1 black, 2 pink, 1 black
> row B: 1 black, 1 pink, 1 black
> row C: 1 black

Twist the ends of wire C together and trim off the extra wire. Repeat ear instructions on wire D to make the second ear.

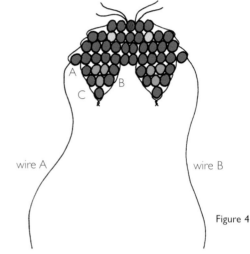

Figure 4

5. String the following rows of beads onto wires A and B (Fig. 5):

> row 5: 12 black
> row 6: 10 black
> row 7: 8 black
> row 8: 11 black

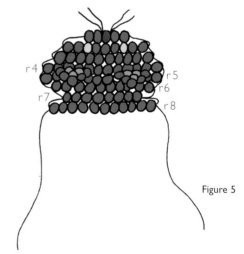

Figure 5

6. To make a front paw, add 6 black beads to wire A. With the same wire, string back through the first bead you added in the opposite direction (Fig. 6). Repeat paw instructions on wire B to make the second front paw.

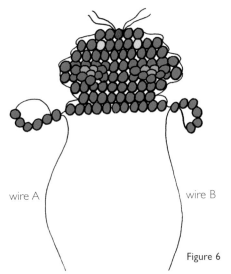

Figure 6

7. Add the following rows of beads to wires A and B in the usual way (Fig. 7):

row 9: 12 black
row 10: 14 black
row 11: 15 black
row 12: 15 black

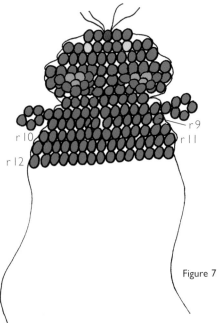

Figure 7

8. To make a back paw, add 7 black beads to wire A, stringing back through the first bead with the same wire (Fig. 8). Repeat on wire B to make a second back paw.

wire A   wire B

Figure 8

9. Now add the following rows of beads (Fig. 9):

row 13: 14 black
row 14: 11 black
row 15: 8 black

Put the wires together and twist once, close to the center of row 15. With the wires together, add one black bead.

Figure 9

10. Add 15 more black beads to the two wires. String both wires through the last bead again to secure the beads. Then twist the wires around a jump ring and trim off the extra wire (Fig. 10). Use your thumb to push up on the belly to give it shape.

Figure 10

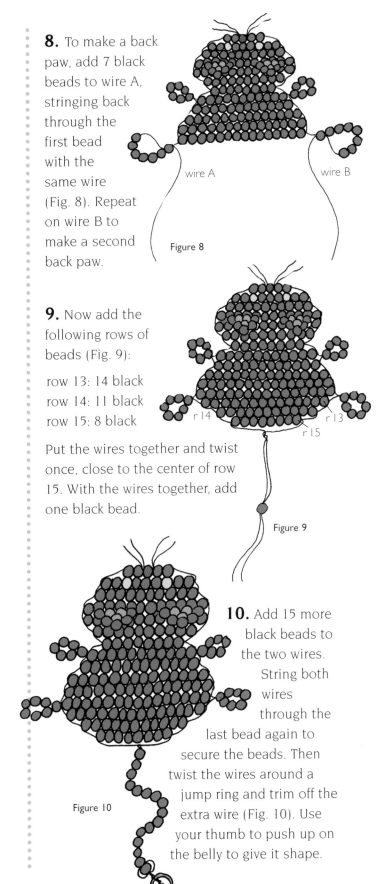

Mouse

Have you ever seen a mouse in your house? House mice originally were found only in Asia, but now live all over the world. Many mice live in the forest, where they eat berries and make nests of soft grasses. Keep this little mouse with you; make it a nest so it can live in your home.

You Will Need

- jump ring
- 36" (91 cm) wire
- two 1" (2.5 cm) wires
- two 5" (12.5 cm) wires
- 5 red e beads
- 14 black e beads
- 122 gray e beads*

*Beads shown are iridescent gray beads

1. Center a jump ring on the 36" wire. One-half of the wire is called wire A. The second half is wire B. String one red bead on wire A, stringing back through the bead with wire B. This will be row 1. String the two 1" wires through the red bead for whiskers (Fig. 1).

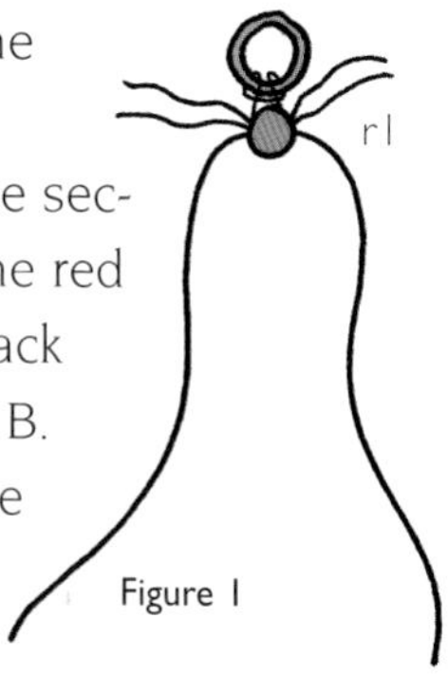

Figure 1

2. String on row 2, 3 gray beads, in the same way (Fig. 2).

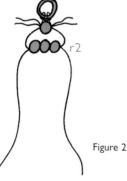

Figure 2

3. String on the following rows of beads (Fig. 3):

row 3: 1 black, 3 gray, 1 black
row 4: 7 gray
row 5: 1 gray, 2 red, 3 gray, 2 red, 1 gray

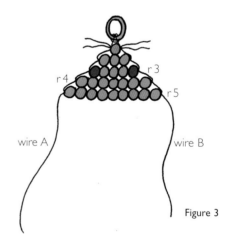

wire A   wire B

Figure 3

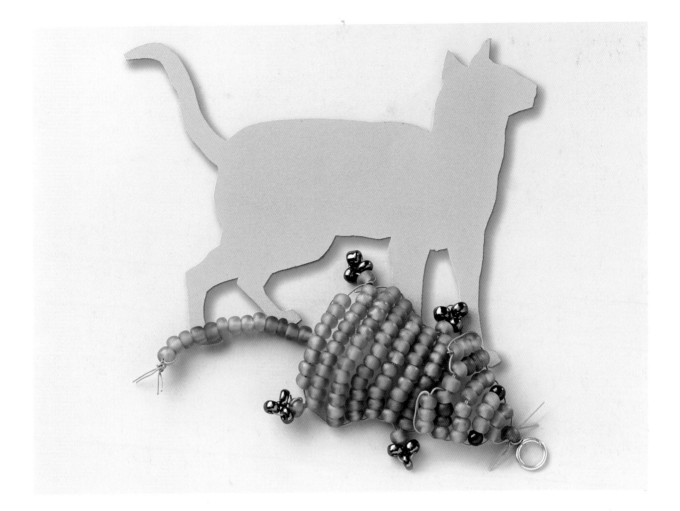

4. String one 5" wire (wire C) so its tails are of even length through beads 1, 2, 3, and 4 of row 5 (Fig. 4). String the other 5" wire (wire D) through beads 6, 7, 8, and 9 of row 5 in the same way.

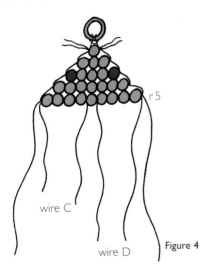

r 5

wire C

wire D

Figure 4

5. To make an ear, add a row of 3 gray beads on one end of wire C, and string back through the beads with the other end of wire C. Twist the ends of the wire together, and trim off the extra wire ends of C (Fig. 5). Repeat on wire D to make the second ear.

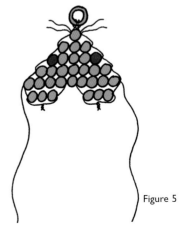

Figure 5

6. Add the following rows of beads to wires A and B (Fig. 6):

> row 6: 7 gray
> row 7: 9 gray

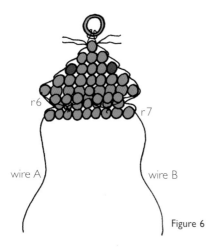

Figure 6

7. To make a front foot, add 1 gray bead and then 3 black beads to wire A, stringing back through the gray bead with wire A in the opposite direction, as shown (Fig. 7). Repeat on wire B to make the second front foot.

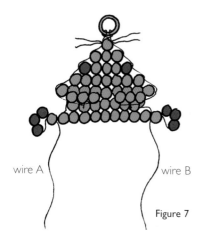

Figure 7

8. Add the following rows of beads (Fig. 8):

> row 8: 9 gray
> row 9: 10 gray
> row 10: 12 gray
> row 11: 14 gray
> row 12: 12 gray

To make a back foot, add 1 gray bead and then 3 black beads to wire A, stringing back through the gray bead with wire A in the opposite direction, as shown (Fig. 8). Repeat on wire B to make the second back foot.

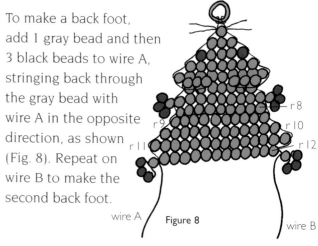

Figure 8

9. String on row 13, 8 gray beads. Bring wires A and B together at the center of row 13 and twist together once (Fig. 9). For the tail, string 13 gray beads on both wires together. String both wires back through the last bead to secure the beads and leave ¼'' (5 mm) of wire, trimming off extra wire. Finally, use your thumb to press up the body of your mouse and give it some shape.

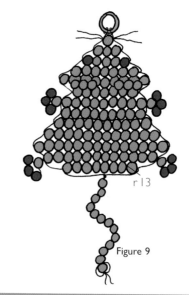

Figure 9

Puppy

The ancestors of man's best friend were wolves. Dogs were first domesticated about 12,000 years ago, perhaps when they started hanging around people's campfires, looking for food. This playful puppy can tag along wherever you go.

You Will Need

- jump ring
- 36" (91 cm) wire
- 22 amber e beads
- 168 dark brown e beads
- 3 black e beads

This pattern starts at the tail and works up towards the nose.

1. Center a wire on a jump ring. We will call one-half wire A and the other half wire B. String one dark brown bead on wire A. String wire B back through the bead in the opposite direction to make row 1 (Fig. 1).

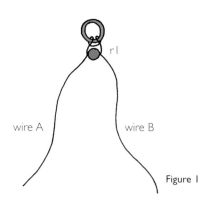

Figure 1

2. In the same way, add the following rows of beads (Fig. 2):

row 2: 2 dark brown
row 3: 2 dark brown
row 4: 2 dark brown
row 5: 8 dark brown
row 6: 10 dark brown

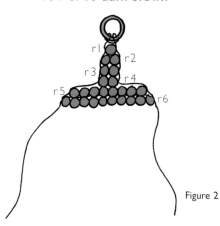

Figure 2

3. To make a back leg, string 7 dark brown beads on wire A, stringing back through the first bead as shown (Fig. 3). Repeat on wire B to make the second back leg.

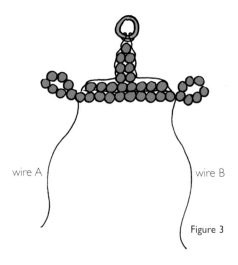

Figure 3

4. Add the following rows of beads (Fig. 4):

row 7: 11 dark brown
row 8: 12 dark brown
row 9: 11 dark brown
row 10: 10 dark brown
row 11: 9 dark brown

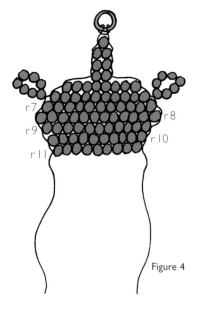

Figure 4

5. To make a front foot, add 7 dark brown beads to wire A, stringing back through the first 2 beads with the same wire as shown (Fig. 5). Repeat on wire B for the second front foot.

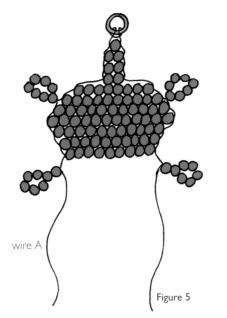

wire A

Figure 5

6. Add the following rows of beads (Fig. 6):

  row 12: 9 dark brown
  row 13: 8 dark brown
  row 14: 5 dark brown
  row 15: 5 dark brown
  row 16: 7 dark brown

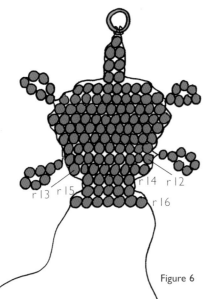

Figure 6

7. For the ear, add 11 amber beads to wire A, stringing back through the first bead as shown (Fig. 7). Repeat on wire B for the second ear.

Figure 7

8. Add the following rows of beads to finish Fig. 8):

  row 17: 2 dark brown, 1 black, 1 dark
    brown, 1 black, 2 dark brown
  row 18: 7 dark brown
  row 19: 5 dark brown
  row 20: 1 black

String the wires back through this last black bead to secure the beads, and trim off the excess wire. Finally, use your thumb to push up the body of the puppy and give it some shape.

Figure 8

Bunny

In ancient Mexico, the Mayan people saw a leaping rabbit in the full moon, rather than the Man in the Moon. Look at the moon when it is full. What do you see? Meanwhile, here's a little bunny for you to make.

The pattern is worked from the tail back. The bunny's ears are floppy.

1. Center the 36" wire on a jump ring. One-half is wire A; the other half is wire B. String on 5 white beads to each wire (Fig. 1).

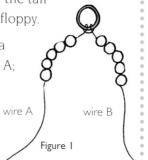

wire A   wire B

Figure 1

2. String wire A back counter-clockwise through the beads on wire B and then through the beads on wire A again, and pull tight (Fig. 2).

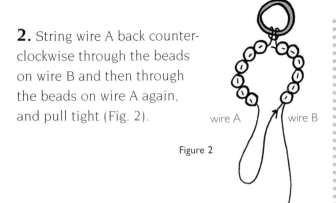

Figure 2

3. Add the following rows of beads (Fig. 3):

row 1: 8 white
row 2: 11 white
row 3: 14 white

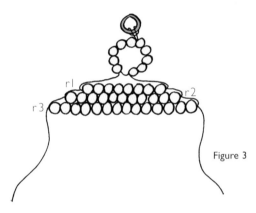

Figure 3

4. To make a back foot, add 6 white beads to wire A, stringing back through the first bead with the same wire, as shown (Fig. 4). Repeat on wire B to make the second back foot.

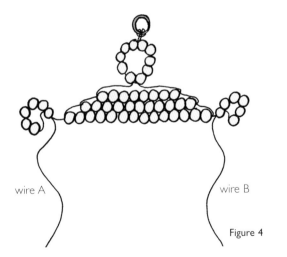

Figure 4

5. Add the following rows of beads (Fig. 5):

row 4: 16 white
row 5: 15 white
row 6: 14 white
row 7: 12 white
row 8: 11 white

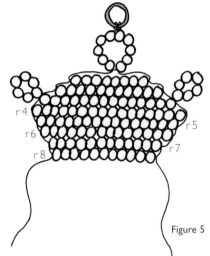

Figure 5

6. To make a front foot, add 6 white beads to wire A, stringing back through the first bead with the same wire, as shown (Fig. 6). Repeat on wire B to make the second front foot.

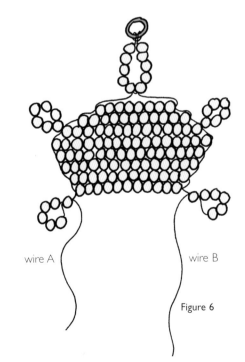

Figure 6

7. Add the following rows of beads (Fig. 7):

row 9: 8 white

row 10: 10 white

row 11: 11 white

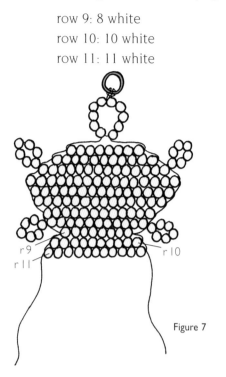

Figure 7

8. To start the ears, string one of the 6″ wires (wire C) through beads 2, 3, and 4 of row 11 (Fig. 8) so the wire ends are of even length. String the other wire (wire D) through beads 8, 9, and 10 of row 11. (Just leave the ends of wires A and B alone for now.)

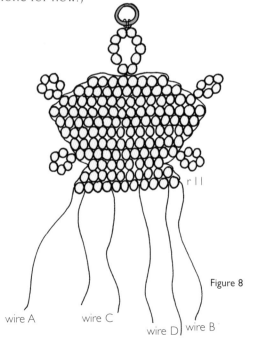

r 11

Figure 8

wire A   wire C   wire D   wire B

9. To make an ear, add rows of beads to one end of wire C, stringing back through the beads with the second end of wire C (Fig. 9):

row A: 1 white, 1 pink, 1 white

row B: 1 white, 1 pink, 1 white

row C: 1 white, 2 pink, 1 white

row D: 1 white, 2 pink, 1 white

row E: 1 white, 1 pink, 1 white

row F: 2 white

Put the two ends of wire C together close to row F, twist twice, and trim off the excess. To make the second ear, make rows A to F on wire D in the same way; twist the wire ends together and trim.

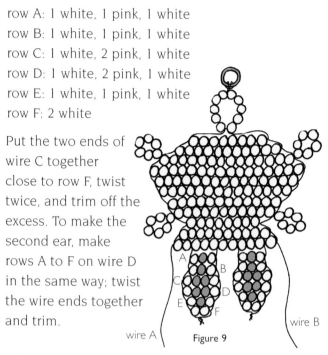

wire A   Figure 9   wire B

10. On wires A and B, add the following rows of beads to finish the face (Fig. 10):

row 12: 3 white, 1 black, 3 white, 1 black, 3 white

row 13: 3 white, 1 red, 3 white

Put the wire ends together near the center of row 13, twist to secure, and trim off the extra wire. String both 2″ wires through the red bead to make whiskers. Trim the whiskers back, push up with your thumb to give your bunny's belly some shape.

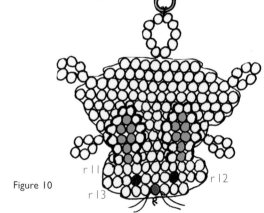

Figure 10   r 11   r 12   r 13

Camel

Camels live in North Africa and Asia. They can go long distances without water. Maybe your camel will enjoy traveling with you.

You Will Need

- jump ring
- 40'' (102 cm) wire
- 3'' (7.5 cm) wire
- 157 gold e beads
- 1 black e bead
- 8 dark brown beads
- 18 gold seed beads

The rows for the camel will be vertical.

1. String 3 gold e beads onto the center of the 40'' wire. One-half of the wire is called wire A. The other half is wire B. String back through the 3 beads with one-half of the wire as shown (Fig. 1). This starts the head.

Figure 1

2. Add the following rows of e beads by stringing each row on wire A and then stringing back through each row with wire B (Fig. 2):

 row 2: 4 gold
 row 3: 4 gold
 row 4: 1 black, 4 gold
 row 5: 6 gold
 row 6: 6 gold

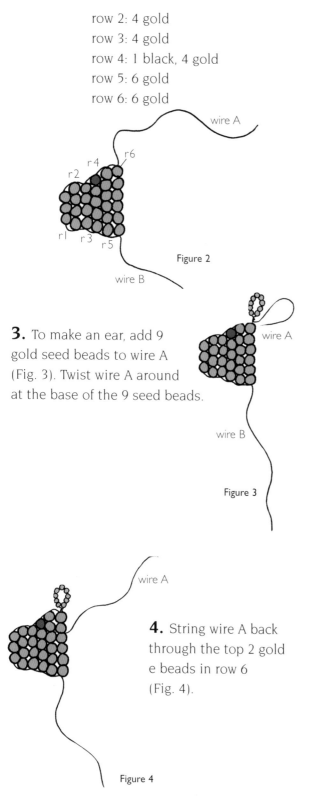

Figure 2

3. To make an ear, add 9 gold seed beads to wire A (Fig. 3). Twist wire A around at the base of the 9 seed beads.

Figure 3

4. String wire A back through the top 2 gold e beads in row 6 (Fig. 4).

Figure 4

5. To make the second ear, add 9 gold seed beads to wire A. Twist wire A around the base of the 9 seed beads, and then string wire A through the last 4 gold e beads in row 6 (Fig. 5).

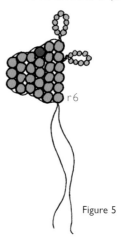

Figure 5

6. Put the wires together and string 8 gold e beads for the neck (Fig. 6).

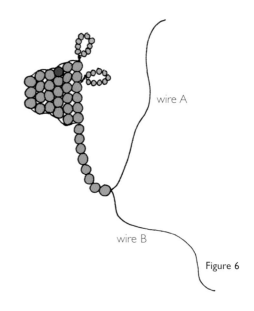

Figure 6

7. To add row 7, separate the wires and add 7 gold e beads to wire B. String wire A back through the 7 e beads in the opposite direction, but keep the neck of the camel lined up with the lowest bead in row 7 (Fig. 7).

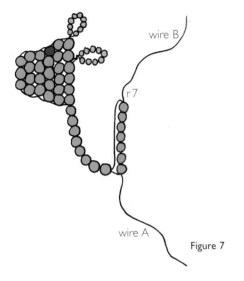

Figure 7

8. To make a leg, separate the wires and add 6 gold e beads to wire A and then 2 dark brown e beads. Run wire A back through the 6 gold e beads you just added (Fig. 8).

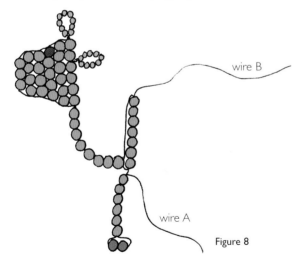

Figure 8

9. To make another leg, add 6 more gold e beads and 2 dark brown e beads to wire A. Run wire A back through the gold e beads (Fig. 9).

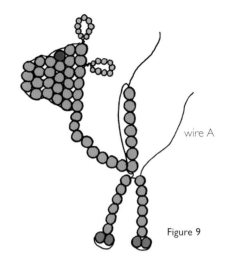

Figure 9

10. Add 9 gold beads for row 8 (Fig. 10) in the same way you added row 7.

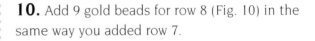
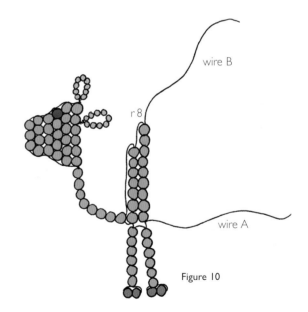

Figure 10

11. Add the following rows of e beads in the same way (Fig. 11):

> row 8: 9 gold
> row 9: 11 gold
> row 10: 13 gold
> row 11: 14 gold
> row 12: 13 gold
> row 13: 10 gold
> row 14: 8 gold

To make a leg, separate the wires and add 6 gold beads and then 2 dark brown beads to wire A, stringing the wire back through the 6 gold e beads (Fig. 11). Add 6 more gold e beads and 2 dark brown beads to wire A, stringing back through the 6 gold e beads with wire A again, to make a second leg.

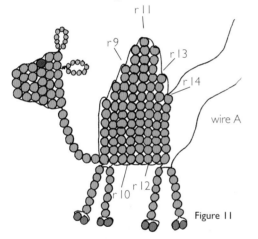

Figure 11

12. Add row 15, 6 gold e beads (Fig. 12) on wire B, stringing back through them with wire A.

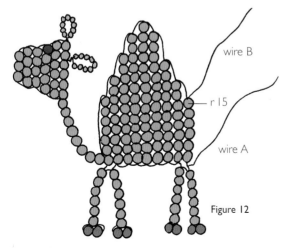

Figure 12

13. String wire A back through all but the first gold e bead of row 15 (Fig. 13). Bring the wires together and string on 7 gold e beads for a tail, stringing the wires back through the last e bead to secure. Trim off the excess wire, leaving ¼'' (5 mm) wire ends.

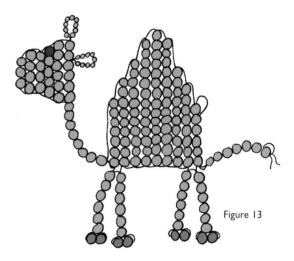

Figure 13

14. Finally, string the 3'' wire through the top bead in row 11, or through the wires on either side of it. Fold the wire in half and twist the ends together close to the same bead. Then twist the ends around a jump ring and trim off the extra wire.

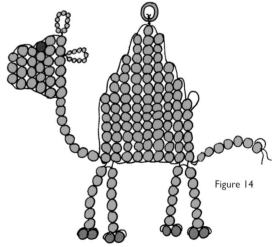

Figure 14

About the Author

Photo by Kimio Honda

Sonal Bhatt was born and raised in Framingham, Massachusetts. Her parents immigrated to the United States from Gujarat, India, where beading is a traditional art form. She developed her love of all things crafty from her mom, who taught her that the best use of spare time is to be creative.

Sonal is trained as a marine biologist and works as an exhibit developer, connecting science, nature, and art and creating learning experiences for families through hands-on activities. She is currently working for a conservation organization, designing exhibits for zoos, aquariums, and museums.

Sonal is trained in the traditional Indian classical dance form of Bharatanatyam. She is always working to find ways to wed her Indian heritage and her experiences of growing up in the United States through the arts and dance.

Beaded Critters is Sonal's second book. She also wrote *Totally Beads*, published in 2001, a creative guide to making beaded jewelry. She currently resides in New York City.

Index

FEB   2006